THE CATHEDRAL CHURCH OF LINCOLN

A HISTORY AND
DESCRIPTION
OF ITS FABRIC AND A LIST
OF
THE BISHOPS

BY A. F. KENDRICK

GENERAL PREFACE

This series of monographs has been planned to supply visitors to the great English Cathedrals with accurate and well illustrated guide-books at a popular price. The aim of each writer has been to produce a work compiled with sufficient knowledge and scholarship to be of value to the student of Archæology and History, and yet not too technical in language for the use of an ordinary visitor or tourist.

To specify all the authorities which have been made use of in each case would be difficult and tedious in this place. But amongst the general sources of information which have been almost invariably found useful are:—(1) the great county histories, the value of which, especially in questions of genealogy and local records, is generally recognised; (2) the numerous papers by experts which appear from time to time in the Transactions of the Antiquarian and Archæological Societies; (3) the important documents made accessible in the series issued by the Master of the Rolls; (4) the well-known works of Britton and Willis on the English Cathedrals; and (5) the very excellent series of Handbooks to the Cathedrals originated by the late Mr John Murray; to which the reader may in most cases be referred for fuller detail, especially in reference to the histories of the respective sees.

|iv|

AUTHOR'S PREFACE

The literature on the subject of Lincoln Minster is considerable, but scattered. The valuable researches of the late Precentor Venables published chiefly in the *Archæological Journal*, claim the first place among authorities consulted in the preparation of the present handbook. The works of Freeman, Scott, Rickman, and Parker have also been referred to. For the Episcopal Visitations, Prebendary Perry's account in the thirty-eighth volume of the *Archæological Journal* has been followed; and for the Inventories of the Treasures, that of Prebendary Wordsworth in the fifty-third volume of the *Archæologia*. Holinshed's "Chronicles," Bright's "Early English Church History," and the topographical works of Leland, Dugdale, Camden, and Stukeley, contain useful information on the subject. In the Rolls series, the chronicles of Henry of Huntingdon, Matthew Paris, Roger de Hoveden, and Giraldus Cambrensis, as well as the annals of various reigns and the "Magna Vita" of St. Hugh, have been consulted. A number of old guides in the Library of the British Museum contain useful MS. notes. Some of the other works referred to have been acknowledged in the pages of this book.

The author has to acknowledge his indebtedness to Mr J. Shillaker and Mr G. H. Palmer for kind suggestions. Mr P. G. Trendell has prepared the list of the Bishops, and has given valued help in other ways. The illustrations are largely taken from photographs reproduced by the kindness of the Photochrom Co., Messrs S. B. Bolas & Co., Mr F. G. M. Beaumont, and Mr H. C. Oakden; others are from the Lincoln volume of the Proceedings of the Archæological Institute (1848).

A. F. K.

May 1898.

|v|

LINCOLN CATHEDRAL
CHAPTER I
THE HISTORY OF THE BUILDING

The venerable walls of Lincoln Minster look down from their proud position upon a city far more ancient than themselves. Long before the arrival of the Saxons and Angles, the spot on which Lincoln Minster and Castle stand, had been occupied by a settlement bearing a name which has survived through various changes to the present day. "Lincoln" is "Lindum Colonia": the latter word dates from the Roman occupation of Britain, and is sufficient to show the importance of the city at such an early period; the former carries us back further still to the times of the ancient Britons, whose dwelling on the "dun" or hill, was named "Llin-dun," from the "llin" or mere at its foot. The hill is that on which the minster now stands, and the mere still survives in the harbour of Brayford. The limits of the Roman city on the summit of the hill were marked by massive quadrangular walls, of which fragments may be seen at the present day. These walls were pierced with four gates; the position of the east and west gates is marked by the streets bearing these names; the southern gateway was still in existence at the beginning of the eighteenth century, but was battered down by a man named Houghton about the year 1707. The old Roman road to the north still passes under the northern or "Newport" gate.

The city occupied a proud position, and its importance in Roman times is shewn by the fact that it was the meeting-point of five main roads, two of which, the Foss Way and Ermine Street, met a little south of the present church of St. Botolph, and formed what is now the High Street of the [4]city. Remains of Roman Lincoln are abundant, and some are preserved within the minster precincts. Passing on to the time of the Saxons, we read that the indefatigable missionary Paulinus, Bishop of York, journeyed into the neighbouring district of Lindsey, and "preached in the old Roman hill-town of Lincoln." His labour was rewarded by the conversion (about the year 628) of its "prefect" Blaecca, who immediately set about building "a stone church of noble workmanship" for the use of the converts to the new faith. But it is not directly to the preaching of Paulinus, nor to the energy of Blaecca, that we owe the foundation of the minster. The "stone church" is now almost certainly represented by the church of St. Paul, in Bailgate, a church which still retains the name, though in a corrupted form, of the first great Christian missionary to the people of Lincoln. In this church Honorius was consecrated by Paulinus to succeed Justus as Archbishop of Canterbury. The little village of Stow, eleven miles to the north-west of the city, has been identified by Professor Freeman as "the ancient Sidnacester," and can thus claim to be the original seat of the diocese of Lincoln. The venerable church of St. Mary at Stow was called by Camden "the mother-church to Lincoln." In the year 678, when the huge Northumbrian diocese of Wilfrid was divided, Egfrid of Northumbria built a church at Sidnacester. This church was made the "bishopstool" of the new diocese of Lindsey, and the line of bishops may be traced for two hundred years, from Eadhed to Berhtred. During the bishopric of the latter, about the year 870, the church at Stow was burnt in an invasion of the Northmen, and in consequence of their ravages the see remained vacant for a period of eighty years. Lincoln itself fell into the hands of the invaders, and became the chief of the "Five Boroughs" of the Danish Confederation. From this time until the Norman invasion the borough continued to be governed by its twelve hereditary Danish law-men. About the middle of the tenth century, the seat of the bishops of this district was removed for security to Dorchester-on-Thames, in the very farthest corner of the vast diocese, where it was protected by the fortified camp. The Mercian see of Leicester was here united with that of Sidnacester, and in the next century Eadnoth, the second of the name, is styled Bishop [5]of Dorchester, Leicester, and Sidnacester. The little city by the Thames was not long to enjoy the honour of being the "bishopstool" of the largest diocese in England. As the Saxons gave way before their Norman conquerors, the Saxon bishop of Dorchester was succeeded by the Norman bishop of Lincoln. William the Conqueror brought many prelates in his train, and not the least conspicuous among them was Remigius, who was destined soon to share largely in the spoils of the newly-conquered country. This man was Almoner of Fécamp on the coast of Normandy. His offer, for the projected invasion, of a single ship with twenty knights, procured him the promise of the first English bishopric vacant, and the Conqueror redeemed his word on the death of Wulfwig, Bishop of Dorchester. In the first years of his episcopate, Remigius commenced to build on a stately scale at Dorchester, but it seemed to him inconvenient, so Henry of Huntingdon records, that the see should be in a corner of the diocese. Remigius had already begun to look on the "distinguished city of Lincoln" as being more worthy to be the seat of a bishop, when in the year 1072 a council held at Windsor decreed that bishops should fix their sees in walled towns instead of villages. Remigius would naturally turn to the district of Lindsey, whence his predecessors had come, and with his choice of Lincoln begins the history of our minster. The city at this time, according to the Domesday record, boasted eleven hundred and sixty inhabited houses. The Conqueror, "in feare of rebellious commotions," had already commenced the erection of a castle there to overawe the surrounding country. For this purpose, one hundred and sixty-six houses were destroyed on the top of the hill, within the bounds of the Roman walls. Their inhabitants were driven beyond the Witham to found a new town in the plain beneath, where the land belonged to Coleswegen, an English favourite of the king. The towers of St. Mary-le-Wigford and St. Peter-at-Gowts stand to this day as the venerable relics of the churches built by him for these new tenants of his estate. They are extremely valuable records, being monuments of the earlier—Saxon—style of architecture, reared by Englishmen, while the castle and cathedral in the more advanced Norman style were rising on the height above.

The following is Henry of Huntingdon's account of the [6]transference of the see, translated by Precentor Venables:—"The king" (William the Conqueror) "had given Remigius who had been a monk at Fescamp the bishopric of Dorchester which is situated on the Thames. This bishopric being larger than all others in England, stretching from the Thames to the Humber, the bishop thought it troublesome to have his episcopal see at the extreme limit of his diocese. He was also displeased with the smallness of the town, the most illustrious city appearing far more worthy to be the see of a bishop. He therefore bought certain lands on the highest parts of the city, near the castle standing aloft with its strong towers, and built a church, strong as the place was strong, and fair as the place was fair, dedicated to the Virgin of Virgins, which should both be a joy to the servants of God, and as befitted the time unconquerable by enemies." The transference of the see must have taken place between 1072 and 1075, since at the council held in the former year at Windsor, Remigius signed himself "Episcopus Dorcacensis," and three years later at the council of London "Episcopus Lincolniensis." Lincoln thus became the centre of a diocese comprising an enormous area, including the ten following counties:—Lincoln, Northampton, Rutland, Leicester, Cambridge, Huntingdon, Bedford, Buckingham, Oxford and Hertford. In the strong city beneath the massive walls of William's castle, Remigius could build in safety, not hindered, as his predecessors at Stow had been, by the fear of fierce invaders from across the sea.

The piece of ground purchased by Remigius lay a few hundred yards to the east of William's castle, just within the Roman wall of the upper city. It was the site of an earlier church, dedicated to St. Mary Magdalene, which was no doubt entirely destroyed to make room for the prouder edifice of Remigius, and for the next 250 years, the parishioners of St. Mary Magdalene retained the right of assembling in the nave of the minster. The building thus served a double purpose until the time of Bishop John de Dalderby (1300-20), who completed the arrangements begun by his predecessor for the union of the parish of St. Mary Magdalene with that of All Saints.

[7]

OLD MAP OF LINCOLN.
(From Stukeley's *Itinerarium Curiosum*, 1722.)

[8]
The church of Remigius was cruciform, with a short eastern limb, terminating in a semi-circular apse, which, unlike those of Norwich and Gloucester, was destitute of aisles. In the west front, with its three deep and lofty arches, and its two niche-like recesses, we still see the work of the first bishop, but the structure has been twice extended in an easterly direction—once by Bishop Hugh of Avalon, who built the present choir; and the second time to receive that bishop's miracle-working relics, and to afford room for the large and increasing throng of pilgrims that visited his shrine. The existing portions of the fabric built by Remigius are the west front, part of the first bay of the nave, and the side walls now enclosed in Early English chapels. The black basalt font in the nave is of the same period. On the erection of St. Hugh's choir, at the end of the twelfth century, the whole eastern limb of the original structure was removed. But the foundations remained, and were discovered in 1852 by Mr. T. J. Willson, architect, of Lincoln, under the floor of the present choir. The apse was found to have extended a little way beyond where the litany-stool now stands in the choir. The foundations of the lateral walls were also laid bare for some distance. Just beyond the springing of the apse on the north side, there are traces of a pilaster buttress, and on the inside of the lateral walls, sixteen feet from the springing of the apse, the foundations still exist of the piers of the great transverse arch which divided the presbytery from the choir of the Norman church. The measurement of these foundations, as well as the still-existing west front, are sufficient to show the sturdy strength of the early church. The walls of the apse must have been about eight feet thick. There appears to have been a lantern of some kind over the crossing, since the tower which fell in 1237-9 was called *Nova turris*.

The edifice was begun and completed by the energetic bishop, and was ready for consecration within twenty years of its commencement. To judge from the portions yet remaining, the building must have been severely plain; not a moulding softens down the rugged edges in those parts which are still as Remigius left them. But it was solid and strong, built to stand the wear and tear of many centuries. In fact, so like a fortress was it, that Stephen used it as such fifty years after, when the castle opposite was held by his enemies. Precentor Venables thus gives the dimensions of Remigius' church—300 feet in interior length, 160 feet less [9]than at present; 28 feet in breadth, as against 38 feet at present, and 60 feet in height to the level of the ceiling. The roof was undoubtedly of wood, and probably a flat one of painted boards, like those of the transepts at Peterborough. The contemporary church at Canterbury, built by the primate Lanfranc, was roofed in this way. The present nave is 82 feet high, and the choir 74 feet; the comparison of these dimensions with those already given shew that the old church was in every way smaller. And this is only natural. In Norman churches, the stalls for the choir and clergy were usually placed under the lantern or in the first bays of the nave, as at Westminster, Norwich, Winchester and other places. For this and for other reasons the naves were long. The eastern limbs, however, were short, and it remained for later builders to extend them for the transference of the stalls to this part, and to erect Lady Chapels beyond.

Remigius was not destined to witness the consecration of the cathedral he had reared. At the council of Windsor in the year 1072, Thomas, archbishop of York, had laid claim to a jurisdiction over the diocese of Lindsey, which claim had been disallowed. When the question of the consecration of the new cathedral arose, Thomas renewed his pretensions, and the ceremony was thus delayed. We learn from Roger de Hoveden that Remigius, feeling the day of his death draw near, wished to have the church consecrated as soon as possible, and that Rufus was finally won over by a sum of money from the bishop. A date was fixed, the 9th of May, 1092, and all the bishops throughout the country were summoned to be present for the occasion. But on Ascension-day, three days before, Remigius died. He was buried in his own church, before the Altar of the Holy Cross, which stood in front of the screen that carried the rood. The character of the energetic bishop is given in a few words by the historian Henry of Huntingdon—small in stature, but great of heart, swarthy in colour, but comely in deeds (*statura parvus, sed corde magnus, colore fuscus, sed operibus venustus*). His successor was Robert Bloet, Chancellor to William Rufus, but Thomas of York objected to his consecration as bishop of Lincoln. "He might be Bishop of Dorchester, like his predecessors; but Lindesey, part of the spiritual conquest of Paulinus, was of ancient right subject [10]to the metropolitan authority of York. This claim came to nothing, and Thomas found better scope for his energies in the reform of his own church." 1 A present from Bloet of £5000 to the king set matters right, and the ceremony so long delayed was at last performed. The bishop does not appear to have made any addition to the fabric before his death, which occurred suddenly, while riding with the king in a "deer-fold" at Woodstock (10th January 1123). It was quite otherwise with his successor, Alexander the Magnificent, nephew of the princely Roger of Salisbury. Alexander had already shewn his love of building by the erection of strong castles at Newark, Banbury and Sleaford, when a fire which destroyed the roof of the cathedral about the year 1141, gave him an opportunity of exercising his talent in a direction more fitting to his office. Giraldus Cambrensis relates that in this fire the burning beams fell from the roof and broke the slab of Remigius' tomb. This fact is interesting as adding support to the opinion that the slab now replaced in the nave of the minster was really that which covered the original burial-place of the bishop. Of the stone vaulting with which Alexander replaced the wooden roof after the fire, not a fragment remains; but the lines of the vault may be traced at the western end of the nave and against the two west towers. In addition to this, we learn from Henry of Huntingdon that he so remodelled the church by his "subtle artifice," that it looked more beautiful than in "its first newness," and was not surpassed by any building in England. The difference between the work of Remigius and Alexander is well seen in the west front, where the three great uncompromising arches of the earlier bishop are pierced by the rich and elaborate doorways of the later. We are fairly safe in assigning these to Alexander, and they probably formed part of the work he did, according to Roger de Hoveden, in the year 1146. The intersecting

Norman arcade along the west front, just above the work of Remigius, may also be ascribed to Alexander, as well as the lower portions of the two western towers. The connection of these towers with the original west front was unfortunately hidden by the erection of the present Gothic screen-wall. It will be noticed, however, that gables are [11]added at the sides to the Norman work, and traces may be seen which prove that similar gables decorated their western faces. There was probably another gable of larger dimensions in the centre. Precentor Venables thus conjectured the appearance of the west front as begun by Remigius and completed by Alexander: "It was furnished with three gables, like the façade of the cathedral of Ferrara, behind which rose the low Norman towers still existing, richly ornamented with three tiers of arcades, ... and terminated with low spires of timber covered with lead, similar to those which once covered the western towers of Durham, or those still nearer, which have recently been replaced, with happy effect, at Southwell. The angular turrets would also be terminated in a similar manner, giving a picturesque combination of spires."

In the time of the "magnificent" bishop, Lincoln was the scene of stirring events, in which the minster played a curious part. The lamentable war between Stephen and Matilda produced a miserable state of confusion and bloodshed in every corner of the land. The strong castle of Lincoln was seized by William de Roumara, Earl of Lincoln, and Ranulph, Earl of Chester, and held for Matilda. The citizens and Bishop Alexander sent word to the king, who hastened to their relief. The king's eye fell on the massive walls of the minster, in such a convenient position opposite the stronghold of the earls. The sacred fabric was seized, and, according to William of Malmesbury, garrisoned as a fortress. Such a proceeding could bring no good fortune to the king, and omens of evil soon followed. As he offered a wax candle in the minster, Henry of Huntingdon tells us, it broke just when Bishop Alexander was about to take it. The chain too, by which the pyx was suspended, snapped asunder, and the sacred vessel fell, in the presence of the bishop. The decisive contest took place soon after; Stephen was left a captive in the hands of his enemies, and the city was taken and plundered. Two years before these events, in 1139, Alexander and his uncle Roger, bishop of Salisbury, had been treacherously seized by the king, and deprived of their treasures and castles. Roger died insane at the end of the same year, and Alexander regained his liberty on resigning his castles.

[12]

In 1144 Stephen was again at Lincoln, besieging the castle, where his enemies repulsed every attack. Two years later, at Christmas time, the king appeared crowned within the city, in defiance of an ancient superstition which foretold evil to any English sovereign who should do so. Eleven years after, Henry II. out of deference to this tradition, was crowned outside the walls, in the suburb of Wikeford. In 1167, on the death of Bishop Chesney, the king seized the revenues, and the see remained vacant for many years. A prophecy that it would never again be filled seemed likely to prove true, when Geoffrey Plantagenet, a natural son of the king, was elected in 1173. He was never consecrated, and resigned nine years later. During his term of office, Geoffrey gave to the minster "two great sonorous bells," which were probably hung in one of the western towers.

SEALS OF WILLIAM DE ROUMARA, EARL OF LINCOLN, AND OF RANULPH, EARL OF CHESTER AND LINCOLN.

The fabric of the church is considered to have remained as left by Alexander until the year 1185. On the 15th April of this year occurred the great earthquake mentioned by Roger de Hoveden. He tells us that it was felt throughout almost the whole of England, and was of such a severity as had not been known in the land "*ab initio mundi.*" The minster was cleft from the top to the bottom.

The disasters of this year were more than compensated in the next, when a man was consecrated to the bishopric who [13]has left a name as great as any that figure in the ecclesiastical history of England. St. Hugh of Lincoln was a son of a Lord of Avalon, near Grenoble. At an early age he entered a priory, a dependency of the cathedral church of Grenoble, and near his father's castle and land. About 1160 he was received into the Grand Chartreuse, where he became eventually the procurator or bursar. Henry II. of England, hearing of his fame, sent the bishop of Bath and other ambassadors to the great Carthusian monastery, begging that Hugh should come to England, and take charge of the newly-established monastery of the Carthusians at Witham in Somersetshire. The prior was not at all inclined to part with Hugh, but the matter was settled by the bishop of Grenoble, and Hugh crossed over to England.

SEAL OF HENRY DE LACY, EARL OF LINCOLN.

At Witham Hugh became a great favourite with the king, who, about ten years after his arrival in this country, offered him the vacant bishopric of Lincoln. The prior was not, however, dazzled by the prospect of a bishop's mitre, and the king had to tax his persuasive powers before he could induce him to exchange Witham for Lincoln. When once installed, Hugh, like Thomas of Canterbury, soon made it clear that he would become no tool in the hands of the king. Henry's chief forester was excommunicated for an offence against the church, and Hugh refused to bestow a vacant prebend on a courtier recommended by the king. The bishop was summoned to the royal presence, Henry instructing his courtiers not to salute him when he entered. Hugh found the king sewing a bandage round a wounded finger, and apparently so occupied as not to notice his approach. The bishop, not at all disconcerted, made some witty remark about the king reminding him of his ancestor of Falaise; whereupon Henry burst into laughter, and explained the joke to his courtiers. In the year 1198, in a council held at Oxford, Hugh and the bishop of Salisbury [14]stood alone in opposing a grant for the king's foreign wars; "the saint of Lincoln, grown into an Englishman on English ground, spoke up for the laws and rights of Englishmen." Richard was furious, and ordered the confiscation of his property; but Hugh stood firm, and the king at last gave way. Yet this dignified assertion of his rights was not accompanied by an arrogant spirit. The miracles which, in an ignorant and superstitious age, were attributed to many who had a reputation for piety, were strenuously disclaimed by him. Such was the man who, in 1186, became bishop of the vast diocese of Lincoln.

The building was in a most deplorable state, and Hugh had thus an opportunity of becoming, so to speak, the second founder of the church. He quickly resolved to commence the building entirely afresh from the foundations. The sum of money necessary for this purpose was large, and Hugh proposed to retire to Witham until the accumulated revenues of the see should reach the amount required. Although he was not permitted to do this, he often visited the little Somersetshire monastery, where he would remain for a month or two at a time, doing the duties of a simple monk, and practising all the austerities of the Carthusian order. For six years Hugh diligently collected the materials for carrying out his great scheme, and at last the foundations of a new choir were laid. The year 1192 marks an epoch, not only in the history of Lincoln Minster, and of English architecture, but in that of Gothic architecture generally. "What Diocletian did at Spalato for the round arch, Saint Hugh did at Lincoln for the pointed arch.... We have seen how, while the elder church of Remigius was rising in the stern grandeur of early Norman times, men were still found who clave to the older traditions of independent England. So, while its eastern limb was giving way to the new form which rose at the bidding of Saint Hugh, men were still rearing the naves of Peterborough and Ely, works which shew in their details some signs of the change which was beginning, but which, in their leading lines and proportions, vary not at all from the earlier works which they continue." "St. Hugh was strictly the first to design a building in which the pointed arch should be allowed full play, and should be accompanied by an appropriate system of detail.... To [15]Hugh of Avalon, neither from the West-Saxon nor the Ducal-Burgundian Avalon, ... French and English forms would be alike foreign, and he doubtless gave full play to the taste of his architect, a taste which did nothing less than develop on the soil of Lindesey the first complete and pure form of the third great form of architecture, the architecture of the pointed arch." 2 Who was this architect? What nation did he belong to? These questions are of considerable interest. The first it is easy to answer. In the "*Magna Vita*" of St. Hugh we read that the architect was Geoffrey de Noyers (*Gaufrido de Noiers*). The name certainly looks like that of a foreigner, but from a letter contributed by M. Viollet le Duc to the *Gentleman's Magazine* in May 1861, we must conclude that he was in all respects an Englishman, though doubtless of foreign descent. The letter contains such interesting remarks on the characteristic differences between French and English Gothic, that it may be worth while to quote it in full—

"I expected from what I had heard in England to find at Lincoln the French style of architecture, that is to say, some constructions of the end of the twelfth century and the beginning of the thirteenth which would shew the evident influence of a French architect. But after the most careful examination I could not find in any part of the cathedral of Lincoln, neither in the general design, nor in any part of the system of architecture adopted, nor in the details of ornament, any trace of the French school of the twelfth century (the lay school from 1170 to 1220), so plainly characteristic of the Cathedrals of Paris, Noyon, Senlis, Chartres, Sens, and even Rouen. The part of the cathedral of Lincoln in which the influence of the French school has been supposed to be found, has no resemblance to this. I speak of the choir. On the exterior the choir of the cathedral of Lincoln is thoroughly English, or Norman if you will: one can perceive all the Norman influence; arches acutely pointed, blank windows in the clerestory, reminding one of the basilica covered with a wooden roof; a low triforium; each bay of the aisles divided into two by a small buttress; shafts banded. In the interior, vaults which have not at all the same construction as the French [16]vaults of the end of the twelfth century; arch-mouldings slender, and deeply undercut; the abacus round; the tooth-ornament; which do not at all resemble the ornaments which we find at Paris, Sens, St. Denis, &c.

"As to the large rose window of the north transept, which is said to have been executed between 1190 and 1200, without disputing that date, which appears to me rather an early one for it, I cannot consider it as a French composition. In the first place, I do not know a rose window of that period in France which is divided into four compartments; the centre of this window does not resemble the arrangement adopted in France; and as to the decoration with small roses which cover the mouldings, they are a very characteristic English ornament.

"Nowhere in France do we find between 1190 and 1200 pillars similar to those at Lincoln, with the crockets placed between the shafts; nowhere in France do we find crockets carved like these; nowhere shafts with hexagonal concave section; nowhere capitals or abacus similar to those of these pillars.

MONUMENTAL CROCKET.

"Moreover, I confess that I cannot believe readily in the date of 1190 to 1200 for the different parts of this choir; but that the date of 1220, or 1210 at the earliest, seems to me to agree better with the architectural character. We have in Normandy, especially in the cathedral of Rouen and the church of Eu, architecture of the date of 1190; it is purely French, that is to say, it corresponds exactly with the architecture of the 'Isle de France' except in certain details. At Eu, at the cathedral of Le Mans, at Seez, we have architecture which resembles that of the choir of Lincoln, but that architecture is from 1210 to 1220, it is the Norman school of the thirteenth century. There is, indeed, at Lincoln, an effort at, a tendency to originality, a style of ornament which attempts to emancipate itself; nevertheless the character is purely Anglo-Norman.

"The construction is English, the profiles of the mouldings are English, the ornaments are English, the execution of [17]the work belongs to the English school of workmen of the beginning of the thirteenth century."

Sir G. G. Scott was entirely in agreement with the eminent French authority on this point. And the matter was summed up by Precentor Venables in the following words 3:— "Regarding the choir and eastern transept of Lincoln, as we are fully justified in doing, as an English work, great and peculiar interest attaches to it as the earliest dated example of pure Gothic architecture, without any lingering trace of Transitional feeling; the first perfect development of what is known as the Early English style. Other examples of this style might, it is true, were their dates known, prove to have been earlier in execution. But their exact age is unrecorded, and Lincoln stands the foremost of all whose dates we know. Its fully developed style makes the work at first sight, as Sir G. G. Scott has said, seem almost 'an anachronism,' and has caused some, especially M. Viollet le Duc, to imagine that it must be 'antedated.' But there is no building in England of which the precise age is more certainly known, and of the date of which the evidence is more indisputable. No one has ever doubted the early date of Bishop de Lucy's eastern chapels at Winchester. The commencement of these is placed by Professor Willis on documentary evidence in 1202, only ten years after the foundation of the Lincoln choir, while their character is even more advanced than that which is found at Lincoln. One leading characteristic of advance at Lincoln is the circular abacus of the columns, which is found throughout."

The work of St. Hugh at Lincoln is of such extraordinary importance to the student of architecture, that it may be well to closely follow an eminent authority in tracing the parts which date from this bishop's time. J. H. Parker, who remarked that the architecture of Lincoln Minster was his favourite study for thirty years, carefully investigated the matter, and the results were published in the 43rd volume of the *Archæologia*. He says that "the work of the time of St. Hugh, A.D. 1192-1200, is pure early English Gothic, and is the earliest building of that style in the world. The French have nothing so early, not even in the royal domain, which is usually cried up as the district of the earliest Gothic in [18]the world. The best-informed French archæologists admit that they have nothing of the character of Lincoln for twenty or thirty years after the time of St. Hugh.... The portion of the cathedral (erected by St. Hugh) consists of the choir ... the aisles to it and the smaller or eastern transept, with the apsidal chapels on the eastern side of that, also two bays on each side of the chancel arch in the great transept; but the walls of the eastern side of that transept only—the the two ends with the wheel windows and the western walls of the transept are of later periods. The original work had thin walls only, with flat buttresses on the outside, and one of the elegant wall-arcades on the lower part of the inside, making the wall still thinner." Mr. Parker also considered that the vaults were insertions of subsequent periods, and that the original building had only a timber roof and a flat wooden ceiling, similar to that which remains at Peterborough. "When the vaults were added it was found necessary to make the walls thicker, and this was done by a casing on the inside; but the builders being unwilling to conceal the beautiful wall-arcade, made another similar to it in the lower part of the new inner wall, exactly like the earlier one against which it is built, but in such a manner as not to conceal it. This arrangement is proved by a flat vertical joint up the middle of the wall,... not content with this, when the vaults were inserted the architect also placed vaulting-shafts to help to carry those of the aisles, and these descend to the ground. This accounts for the three shafts one in front of the other, which have so long been a puzzle to architects and to students of architectural history. The walls were further strengthened by solid square buttresses built up against the flat ones; these now strong buttresses receive and support the thrust of the vault of the choir, which is carried over the aisle by flying buttresses, with circular openings over the vault of the aisle, built against the inner flat buttress of the inner wall, which had been sufficient to carry the wooden roof, but would not have carried the vault." It may be well to remark here that some authorities have not agreed with Mr. Parker with respect to the stone vault and the double wall-arcade, but have considered that the intention was from the beginning to construct them as they now are seen.

[19]

In addition to the work still existing, St. Hugh united the north and south limbs of his eastern transept by a most remarkable apse. To learn the character of this work we must again trace the foundations beneath the floor. In the year 1791 the choir and presbytery were repaved, when parts of the foundations of Hugh's apse were discovered. The Rev. John Carter, who was master of the Lincoln Grammar School at the time, made a sketch and notes of the discovery. The drawing was lithographed and published in the "Associated Societies' Reports" for 1857. Far more important revelations were made in 1886, when it became necessary to take up a portion of the pavement at the south-west end of the south aisle of the presbytery. Precentor Venables had long desired an opportunity of investigating on this spot, and readily gave permission to have the pavement removed, at the same time instructing that an effort should be made to find the foundations of the destroyed apse. The work began in November, and in consequence of the discovery of part of the south wall, it was decided to systematically proceed with the investigations. The result was highly satisfactory. A detailed account was published in the *Archæological Journal* for 1887, vol. xliv. From this it appears that the apse was almost in the form of a triangle, of which the apex was cut off by a short wall, so as to form a half-hexagon with two long sides, and a shorter one at the end. In each of the longer sides were two chapels, the walls of one in the form of three-fourths of a circle, having a diameter of 18 feet, and the other, a smaller one, having straight side walls and rounded ends; a half-hexagonal chapel with an internal diameter of 23 feet occupied the centre of the apse at the extreme east. It was at first thought that the smaller chapels at the sides might indicate stair-turrets, which would occupy a similar position to those in the apse at Peterborough, but no trace of the foundations of a newel could be found in either case. The apse extended to the second bay of the present Angel Choir, 48 feet short of its eastern end. Throughout almost the whole of the investigations, only the rude concrete foundations were found remaining, their upper surface being about 16 or 17 inches below the existing pavement; in parts, however, fragments of the walling were also discovered.

The eight years during which Hugh carried on the work [20] were busy ones at Lincoln. Contemporary records enable us to picture him encouraging the workmen by his presence and example, even shewing his zeal by carrying the stones on his own shoulders. He did not live to see his work completed, as Remigius had done. But he had set the example and given the pattern, and the work was continued by his successors until the building was again entire. Hugh had already finished the apse, the eastern transept, the choir, and part of the western transept (*i.e.* the whole eastern portion of the church) when he fell ill. Finding his death approaching, he sent for his architect Geoffrey de Noyers, and enjoined him to hasten the completion of the altar of St. John the Baptist, his patron. He then gave directions for his funeral, and instructions that he was to be buried in the mother-church of his diocese dedicated to the Mother of God, near the altar of St. John the Baptist. The personality of the great bishop comes vividly before us when we read that he also wished his tomb to be placed near the wall, in a convenient place, lest it should be a stumbling-block to those approaching. On the 16th November 1200, Hugh breathed his last, lying, as he had wished, on the bare ground, on a cross of consecrated ashes. "A more self-denying, earnest, energetic, and fearless bishop has seldom, if ever, ruled the diocese of Lincoln, or any other diocese whatever" (*Dimock*). His instructions regarding the funeral were carried out; but such a light as Hugh's could not be hid, and within a century we find his remains enclosed in a costly golden shrine, borne on the shoulders of kings and bishops, and placed at last in a structure erected specially for their reception, "one of the loveliest of human works," the celebrated Angel Choir. The original place of Hugh's burial has been somewhat disputed. The "*Magna Vita*" tells us that he was buried near the altar he had named, "*a boreali ipsius aedis regione*." On the east side of the eastern transept, Hugh had placed four apsidal chapels, two north and two south of the central apse. From the words above quoted, it has been considered that the northernmost of these chapels was the site of his tomb. The chapel was greatly enlarged about twenty years after Hugh's death, by the removal of the apse and the extension of the side walls about 50 feet, the chapel being finished with a square east wall. 4 [21]

[22]This fact would certainly add support to the theory that Hugh was buried here, the enlarged chapel forming a sort of intermediate stage between the narrow apse and the splendid Angel Choir. But Mr. T. J. Willson has pointed out 5 that this place was hardly large enough to be a chapel at all, especially as it had a doorway in the north wall, leading from the common room. He considers that the altar of St. John the Baptist was in the central chapel of the great apse, corresponding to its later position in the Angel Choir, and that the coffin found in the north side of this chapel, when the pavement was removed in the year 1886, was the original tomb of St. Hugh. The words "*a boreali ipsius aedis regione*" would then refer, not to the northern side of the church, but merely to the northern side of the chapel in which the bishop was buried. Mr. Willson's assumption certainly throws light on one difficulty, that the northern chapel was called by Bishop Sanderson and others "*capella beatae Mariae Virginis*." The matter is of no great importance, since neither of the chapels exists as it was at the time of Hugh's burial, and whichever of them contained his remains, it did not hold them long. Roger de Hoveden records that King John, on the day before the funeral, offered a golden chalice at the altar of St. John the Baptist, *quod est in novo opere.*

THE CATHEDRAL IN THE SEVENTEENTH CENTURY.
(From an Old Print.)

Of all the great names connected with Lincoln, none are worthy of higher honour than that of the sainted bishop, whose zeal and energy has left so conspicuous a mark on the present fabric, whose shrine was a continual source of revenue for more than three centuries, and whose memory will be revered as long as the walls of Lincoln Minster shall stand.

Although it is somewhat uncertain where the bishop's body was laid, some interesting details of the ceremony have been recorded. Hugh having died in London, the hearse travelled by road to Lincoln, where it was met by King John himself, attended by a numerous retinue of counts and barons. Three archbishops and thirteen bishops were also present at the ceremony. The body was borne by the king and his nobles to the entrance of the minster, [23]where it was received by the archbishops and bishops, who carried it on their shoulders to the choir. The entombment took place next day (24th November). *O quantus luctus omnium, O quanta lamenta, praecipue clericorum.*

An old legend relates that, at the burial of St. Hugh,
"A' the bells o' merrie Lincoln
Without men's hands were rung,
And a' the books o' merrie Lincoln
Were read without man's tongue;
And ne'er was such a burial
Sin' Adam's days begun."

The work of St. Hugh at Lincoln is chiefly of importance as marking an epoch in the history of Gothic architecture. As the earliest known example of the pointed style carried out consistently in its details, the choir of Lincoln Minster cannot be too carefully studied. Close attention will, of course, make more evident its defects; the stone vault, which has the appearance of being all askew, is especially unsuccessful, but the perfection of the Angel Choir could not be attained all at once, and the faults of the earlier work serve but to emphasise the beauties of the later.

At Hugh's death the work did not lie neglected long, if at all. A letter was issued in December 1205, appealing for help on behalf of the *novum opus* at Lincoln. The "Brotherhood of the Church of Lincoln" was offered to those who would contribute; in this way they became enrolled for a certain number of years among those who were specially named in the prayers of the church. The western transept was completed during the early years of the thirteenth century, and the nave constructed, replacing the Norman work of Remigius. The designers here profited by the experience of the past. The vaulting shews a great improvement, and the whole work is of such superior skill as to earn the high praise of the late Professor Freeman, who says that "there are few grander works in the style of the thirteenth century than Lincoln nave, few that shew greater boldness of construction and greater elegance of detail." The nave appears to have been carried steadily onwards to the completion of the first five bays, at which point a curious irregularity is perceptible. The vault suddenly falls two feet lower, and its axis is turned slightly northwards, ultimately falling in with [24]the old west front. The span of the last two bays is also lessened. Perhaps a slight error was made in the direction of the nave at first, which became more evident as time went on, so as to necessitate the change. It has, however, also been suggested that the first intention may have been to remove the west front of Remigius altogether, and to build another at a somewhat different angle farther westwards. If this was the case, economical reasons probably occasioned the change of design, and secured the preservation of a most interesting relic of Remigius' church. It should be remarked that some authorities consider these narrow bays to be no later than the others, and that the work was carried on at both ends of the nave simultaneously, finally meeting towards the middle. There is no document remaining which records the precise date of the erection of the nave at Lincoln, but it would not be difficult to shew that the first half of the thirteenth century practically covers the whole period of its construction. Very little, if any at all, can have been built before the death of St. Hugh in the year 1200, and it was undoubtedly finished before the Angel Choir was begun in 1255. Precentor Venables mentions that Bishop Hugh de Wells, in his will dated 1233, bequeaths 100 marks to the fabric of his church at Lincoln, as well as all the felled timber of which he might die possessed, through all his episcopal estates. He draws the conclusion that the legacy of so large a quantity of timber points to there being a good deal of roofing going on at the time. A new central tower was also begun about this time; it fell in 1237-9, and was replaced by a third, which still stands.

As the new nave was approaching completion, the bishopric of Lincoln was conferred on a man who was destined to play a part second only to that of St. Hugh in the history of the diocese. It has been said that probably no one had greater influence on English thought and literature for the next two centuries than Robert Grosseteste, the friend of Roger Bacon. It is to Grosseteste that Tyssyngton refers when he speaks of "*Lincolniensis, cujus comparatio ad omnes doctores modernos est velut comparatio solis ad lunam quando eclipsatur.*" Of humble birth, Grosseteste rose to be one of the greatest scholars of his day, and the boldest defender of the rights and liberties of the Church of England. In [25]the first year of his episcopacy (1235) he visited the monastic establishments of his diocese, and found it necessary to remove no fewer than seven abbots and four priors. Such a proceeding was, of course, much resented, but when the bishop meditated a still bolder stroke, and contemplated a Visitation of the cathedral, the opposition was brought to a climax. He says: "In my first circuit some came to me finding fault and saying, 'My Lord, you are doing a thing new and unaccustomed.' To whom I answered 'Every novelty which does good to a man is a blessed novelty.'" Grosseteste wrote a pamphlet in defence of his claim, in answer to which the cathedral body produced a charter, altogether a forgery, purporting to give authority to the dean to govern all things, requiring an appeal to the bishop only if his own discipline failed. The matter was referred to the Pope, and finally decided by a Bull of Innocent IV., in 1245, in the bishop's favour. Amongst his reforms was the suppression of the "execrable custom" known as the "Feast of Fools," when the "House of God" was turned into a "house of joking, scurrility, and trifling." It was enjoined that the minster authorities should "by no means permit to be holden this Feast of Fools, since it is full of vanity and defiled with pleasures, in the church of Lincoln on the venerable feast of the Circumcision of our Lord." But there were troubles to come from higher quarters still; Grosseteste had put his hand to the plough, and was determined not to look back. Six years after his triumph over the chapter, he was temporarily suspended by the Pope for refusing to induct an Italian, ignorant of the English tongue, into a rich benefice in his diocese. In the year 1253, the Pope again required him to appoint an Italian (this time his nephew, Frederick di Lavagna) to a canonry, and he again refused. In spite of a sentence of excommunication for this offence, Grosseteste fearlessly continued his episcopal duties.

EARLY ENGLISH PIER.

[26]

The new nave was completed during this episcopate. It soared high above the west front of Remigius, which had to be patched up in a most unfortunate manner before it could do duty under the altered conditions. The experiment was tried of putting a piece of new cloth upon an old garment, and, so far as appearance was concerned, it was a failure. The old Norman work was surrounded by a huge arcaded wall, dislocating the whole façade from the structure behind, and hiding the lower portions of the western towers. The deep recess in the centre was raised far higher, and finished with a pointed arch. The only piece of honesty about the new front was the gable in the middle, which certainly did follow the line of the roof. The wall was flanked by two octagonal turrets, each surmounted by a statue. Beyond the aisles of the nave, two chapels were erected on either side, enclosing the outside walls of the last bay of Remigius' church and together forming what might almost be called a third transept. On the south side of the minster, the canons' vestry was added to the eastern transept, and the Galilee porch to the western. Lastly, the lower portion of the magnificent central, or "Broad," tower was erected, taking the place of the tower which had fallen soon after Grosseteste's appointment.

Matthew Paris tells us a curious story that one of the canons of the minster was declaiming from the pulpit against the actions of Bishop Grosseteste; as he uttered the words "If we were to be silent, the very stones would cry out for us," the new central tower came crashing down, burying several people in the ruins. This catastrophe he assigns to the year 1239. The Chronicles of the Abbot of Peterborough record the event as occurring in the year 1237. There the accident is ascribed, with far greater probability, to the insecurity of the foundations (*propter artificii insolentiam*). The Annals of Dunstable give the same date as Matthew Paris. The fall of the tower crushed part of the vault of St. Hugh's choir, and injured some of the piers, which had to be reconstructed. We may be quite safe in assuming that the new tower was begun soon after, and the reticulated pattern which covers its lower part, both inside and out, may be taken as a mark of Grosseteste's work. The tower was afterwards made higher, and a timber spire added; but Grosseteste's tower was also finished with a spire of timber and lead; the stump of the [27]central shaft may still be seen in the clock chamber. The ten-sided chapter-house, formerly attributed to St. Hugh, was constructed while the nave was in progress. It bears the characteristics of a later period than St. Hugh's choir, and since it is mentioned in the "Metrical Life of S. Hugh," written between 1220 and 1235, it could not have been erected after the latter date.

The bishop died in 1253, leaving the church again complete, though not quite as it is now. The cloisters had not been erected, nor the towers carried to their full height. The eastern end still retained the apsidal form given to it by St. Hugh, and of the demolition of this part of the building it is now time to speak. The fame of the bishop grew fast, and annually attracted to Lincoln a vast crowd of pilgrims seeking bodily or spiritual benefit. Twenty years after his death, a decree of Pope Honorius III. announced his canonisation, and directed that the body should be removed to a more honourable place. Whether the immediate outcome of this was the extension of the semi-circular chapel at the north-eastern angle of the eastern transept, it is difficult to decide, but it is certain that before very many years had passed the fame of St. Hugh gave rise to the destruction of the apse which he himself had reared, and the demolition of part of the ancient city wall. This apse, did it still exist, would be the most remarkable eastern end of any cathedral in England; the one which replaced it is perhaps the most beautiful. Thus the Angel Choir of Lincoln was erected to contain the shrine of one of Lincoln's noblest bishops, and one of England's greatest saints; whose lowly tomb, placed in a corner at his own desire, for fear of its being in the way, had become the resort of such a vast concourse of pilgrims as to require the transformation of the eastern arm of the minster. In 1255, licence was obtained from Henry III. for the removal of part of the eastern city wall, which stood in the way, and in the next year the Angel Choir was probably begun. The work was carried on so rapidly, that within a quarter of a century the translation took place. The choir "was not, however, fully completed till the fourteenth century was well on its way, The work evidently lagged; episcopal appeals, letters of indulgence, and injunctions to the Rural Deans for its completion were issued by Bishop Oliver Sutton in 1297 and [28]1298, and by Bishop John de Dalderby, at various dates between 1301 and 1314. In 1306 a contract for the '*novum opus*' was entered into between the Chapter and Richard of Stow, or Gainsborough, '*cementarius*,' the plain work to be done by measure, and the carved work and sculpture by the day." 6

Richard of Gainsborough now lies buried in the cloisters of the minster. To those who have visited the Abbey of Crowland, on the southern borders of the county, the following statement by Sir G. G. Scott may be of interest. In speaking of the old ruined western front, he says that the details "are hardly to be surpassed, and are the more interesting as having been evidently the work of the architect of the eastern part of Lincoln Cathedral. Even the stone is from Lincoln" ("Lectures on Mediæval Architecture," vol. i. p. 194).

Like the choir of St. Hugh, the Angel Choir stands at the threshold of a new period in architecture. "The style is the earliest Geometrical, of which the triforium and windows are among the best examples in the world." 7 No hard-and-fast line can be drawn, of course, between the different phases of English Gothic, and when we consider that the period during which the Angel Choir was being built includes the last years of the earliest style, and carries us well into the style which followed, it is not difficult to reconcile the words of two eminent authorities on the subject. Fergusson says that "true geometric (window) tracery is ... seen in perfection in the Angel Choir at Lincoln," whilst in Rickman's book we read that we have here the "richest ... and latest work" of the Early English style. Both writers would undoubtedly agree that it is "one of the most beautiful examples of the best period of English art," "simply perfect in its proportion and details." It may be hardly necessary to remark that the name is due to the beautiful sculptured angels filling the spandrels of the triforium.

The 6th October 1280 was the proudest day in the history of the city. Perhaps never, before or since, has such an august assembly gathered within her walls. The body of the Saint of Lincoln was to be translated to the costly shrine in the centre |29|of the Angel Choir. The ceremony was magnificent. Edward himself was present, and supported on his own shoulder the saint's remains as they were carried to their new resting-place; with him was his beloved queen Eleanor, whose effigy was so soon to be placed beneath the same roof. The king and queen were accompanied by Edmund, Earl of Kent, brother of Edward, and his wife; the Earls of Gloucester and Warwick; the Archbishop of Canterbury; the bishops of Lincoln, Bath, Ely, Norwich, Worcester, Llandaff, Bangor, and St. Asaph; the bishop-elect of Exeter; and two hundred and fifty knights. The shrine, ornamented with gold and silver and precious stones, was raised on a lofty stone pedestal, and about thirty years after was protected by an iron grille, wrought by Simon the Smith. It is recorded that the fastenings of the grille were still to be seen in the pavement at the middle of the last century, but all traces have now entirely disappeared. It must have been soon after the translation that the head was removed from the body, and enclosed in a metal case, enriched with gold and silver and precious stones. A keeper was appointed to guard the precious relic during the day, and two had this charge at night. Yet, in spite of all such precautions, it was stolen from the church in the year 1364; the head was thrown into a field, and the case sold in London for twenty marks. The thieves were robbed of their ill-gotten gains on their way back, and were afterwards convicted of the crime, and hanged at Lincoln. The head was found and restored to the cathedral. The treasurer John de Welburne (d. 1380) either restored the old shrine or made a new one of the same materials. The accounts for many years of the receipts and expenditure at the half-yearly opening, when the relics were exhibited to stimulate the offerings of the faithful, are preserved in the muniment room. At Pentecost 1364 (the year of the theft) the amount received was £36, 2s. 3d., and at Pentecost 1532 it had fallen to £2, 2s. 5d., a sure sign of the decline of relic worship. In the year 1540, this shrine shared the fate of so many other precious relics, finding its way to the melting-pots of King Henry VIII.

By the erection of the Angel Choir, the ground plan of the minster was completed almost as it is now. Since that time, the three towers have been raised to a greater height, |30|the cloisters and library constructed, the minster yard protected by gates, and several alterations made in the details of the main building. In the year of the translation of St. Hugh's remains, Oliver Sutton succeeded Richard de Gravesend as bishop. He removed the canons' stable, which stood in close proximity to the minster, and began the erection of the cloisters, starting the work, as his registrar, John de Schalby tells us, by a gift of fifty marks from his own purse. Since Lincoln was a secular foundation, and was never the church of a monastery, there was no absolute need of the cloisters at all, but it is a pity, since they were undertaken, that the work was not more substantially done. Three walks still remain, after having been strengthened by buttresses, and finally reconstructed, owing to the insecurity of the original foundations; the fourth has quite disappeared, and has been replaced by a most incongruous classical structure, after the design of Sir Christopher Wren. The date of the cloisters can be given approximately; they are mentioned as being in progress in a letter of Bishop Sutton's, dated August 23rd, 1296, and such a flimsy structure would probably not take long to finish. Up to this time the central tower still remained as it had been left by Grosseteste. But in the year 1307 Bishop Dalderby issued letters of indulgence for raising it to a greater height. The work was begun on the 14th March in that year, and was probably completed during the next four years, since in 1311 a question arose regarding the cords for two bells which had been lately hung in the tower. A tall spire of wood, coated with lead, was afterwards added. A Lincoln historian of the early part of the present century assigns this spire to Bishop Dalderby, but little reliance can be placed in his testimony, since he ascribes the companion spires on the west towers to the same bishop, and the upper storeys of these towers were not added until a century later.

During this episcopate occurred the trial of the Knights Templars in the chapter-house. A Bull of Pope Clement V., the creature of the French king, who feared the immense power of the knights, pronounced the suppression of the Order in the year 1309. The cruelties with which this was carried out abroad were avoided in this country. The English Templars were put under custody in London, Lincoln, and [31]York. From Lincoln the larger number were transferred to the Tower of London, but Bishop Dalderby was reluctantly compelled to preside at the trial of the others.

In order to trace the history of the walls and gatehouses protecting the close, it is necessary to go back a few years. Edward I. had, in 1285, received a petition from the canons, praying that the close might be fortified. Their plea was, that it had become positively dangerous to attend the midnight services of the church, owing to the number of evil-doers who thronged the precincts. The licence from the king in the year 1285 to the dean and chapter, giving them permission to erect the close wall, is still preserved at Lincoln. The wall was commenced, and in the thirteenth year of Edward II. (1319), permission was given for the addition of towers. Double gateways were erected to guard the approaches. Before we come to speak of the upper storeys of the western towers, a few less important matters may be recorded. It is not difficult to see that the tracery which fills the round window, "the Bishop's eye," of the southern limb of the great transept, does not accord in style with its surroundings. The flowing lines mark a period subsequent to the geometrical forms of the Angel Choir, and later by more than a century than the wall in which the window is placed. This window and that in the gable above, the latter only to be seen from the outside, must be assigned to about the middle of the fourteenth century. About this time, Lincoln received a treasurer, who has left abiding traces in the minster. John de Welburne has already been mentioned as having restored the precious shrine of St. Hugh. Perhaps the greatest of his benefactions are the present magnificent choir-stalls, the finest examples in the kingdom. He also constructed the vaulting of the central and western towers, and placed over the great west door the respectable row of royal statues. Welburne died in the year 1380; this we learn from a volume relating to his chantry and other foundations, written in 1382. The tracery of the three west windows has been assigned by some to him, and by others to a bishop who lived more than half-a-century later. They may be considered as belonging to the end of the fourteenth century, and mark the entrance into the next stage of Gothic architecture, the Perpendicular. The two western towers, St. Mary's [32]and St. Hugh's, had been awaiting their completion for many years. They were now raised to a height of nearly 200 feet, by the addition of early Perpendicular storeys, constructed immediately above the Norman work of Alexander the Magnificent. These towers, as well as the centre one, were crowned by tall spires of wood, coated with lead. The height of these timber spires was 89 feet from the base to the ball, and another 12 feet to the top of the vane; their fate will be recorded later.

Besides the three west windows, and the upper portions of the western towers, the only other parts of the minster in the Perpendicular style are the three chantry-chapels added to the Angel Choir. The first of these was built by Bishop Fleming (d. Jan. 1430-1), and stands on the north side. Bishop Russell (d. 1494) added another opposite to it on the south side. The third chapel was constructed by Bishop Longland (d. 1547). It is a copy of Bishop Russell's, and stands on the same side of the choir, to the west of the doorway. The old library, of which a fragment only remains, was erected in the year 1442 over the east walk of the cloisters. In the year 1609 it suffered severely from fire, and in 1789 all that remained was taken down, with the exception of the part forming a vestibule to the new library.

Turning from the building itself to the internal history of the minster, we find that, towards the middle of the fifteenth century, dissensions had arisen among the cathedral body, which, if not of such historical importance as the differences under Grosseteste, are of sufficient interest to be worth recording. They give considerable insight into the ecclesiastical life of the time. John Mackworth, the dean, was a man of violent temper. In 1435, having some difference with the chancellor, Peter Patrick or Partridge, he entered the church one day during vespers, attended by ten armed servants. The chancellor was dragged from his stall in the choir, brutally assaulted, and left in a wounded condition on the pavement of the church. It is said that over this affair the point was raised during the trial at Westminster, whether the Cathedral Close was in the *county* or the *county of the city* of Lincoln; the delinquents had been described as of the former, and since this was not legally correct, they escaped the punishment they richly deserved. Matters came [33] [34]to a crisis, and the chapter brought before the bishop, William Alnwick, forty-two charges against their dean. The following are sufficient to shew Mackworth's haughty temper:—He would not walk in processions in a straight line; he had fraudulently kept back from the chapter 25s. 8d.; he came to the chapter attended by armed men to the great terror of the canons; at vespers and prime he made the bell stop before the officiating priest had arrived, but made the choir wait for him, if he was late; he had pulled down part of the wall of the cloister to build a stable. The dean in return accused the chapter of appropriating to their own use the cloth bought out of the common funds of the church for clothing the poor. The matter was settled in 1439 by a "Laudum" of the bishop, who set himself the task of constructing a new body of statutes for governing the church; these are still in use. Dissensions, however, did not end here, and we find a complaint made to the bishop four years later, that the dean had, in the choir, called the precentor a "buffoon" and a "vile tailor," and had offered personal violence to him. In 1449 the bishop issued a commission for the trial of the dean, but died before it could take place.

W. Giles, Photo.]

THE WEST FRONT AND THE EXCHEQUER GATE.
(From a Water-colour Painting by Peter De Wint, in the South Kensington Museum.)

Before speaking of the grievous losses which the minster sustained under Henry VIII., it may be well to refer to a Visitation which was undertaken by Bishop Smyth in the first year of the sixteenth century. The charges then brought against the dean, George Fitzhugh, shew the deplorable negligence of the cathedral body with regard to the sacred building under their care. The dean stated that all was right in the cathedral, but from the following statements it would appear that there were several abuses which might with advantage have been corrected. It was affirmed (1) that the chaplains often resorted to a chantry within the church, and there played at dice, bones, and cards in questionable company, often staying till after midnight; (2) that the servants of the dean and other residentiaries did great mischief to the fabric of the church, by breaking the glass windows and the stone tracery with their arrows and crossbow bolts, and by piercing the lead on the roof with their missiles. In the examination that followed it was found that, though large sums had been spent on the fabric, there was still urgent need of further repairs, and an appeal to [35]the public was necessary. We may well be grieved at "the great mischief" done at this time, which would partly account for the dilapidated state of some of the stained glass windows; but the minster was to suffer far more severely under Henry VIII. In the Chapter Acts of 1520 we find mentioned the "head of seint hugh closed in silver gilt and enamelled." The treasure belonging to it is also carefully detailed, down to "a littil blew stone" and "ij qwysshyns of silk." Thus zealously had it been guarded ever since the mishap of 1364, but its doom was now pronounced. At the end of a "Registre and Inventarye of all Jewell Westimentes and other ornamentes in the yere of ow^r lorde god m.ccccc.xxxvj," is "A Copye of the Kinges Lettres by force whereof the shrynes and other Jewels were taken" [1540]. Part of the letter may be given here: "For as moch as we understand that there ys a certain shryne and di[vers] fayned Reliquyes and Juels in the Cathedrall church of Lyncoln with [which] all the symple people be moch deceaved and broughte into greate su[per]sticion and Idolatrye to the dyshonor of god and greate slander of th(is) realme and peryll of theire own soules,

"We Let you wyt that (we) beinge mynded to bringe o^r lovinge subiectes to ye righte knowledge of ye truth by takynge away all occasions of Idolatrye and supersticion. For ye especiall trust (and) confidence we have in yowr fydelytyes, wysdoms and discrecons, have (and) by theis presentes doe aucthorise name assign and appointe you fowre or three of you that immediatelye upon the sighte here of repairinge to ye sayd Cathedrall church and declaringe unto ye Deane Recydencyaryes and other mynisters there(of) the cause of yowr comynge ys to take downe as well ye sayd shryne and supersticious reliquyes as superfluouse

Jueles, plate copes and other suche like as yow shall thinke by yowr wysdoms not mete to contynew (and) remayne there, unto the wych we doubte not but for ye consideraćons rehersed the sayde Deane and Resydencyaryes wthother wyll be conformable and wyllinge thereunto, and so yow to precede accordingly. And to see the sayd reliquyes, Juels and plate safely and surely to be conveyde to owr towre of London in to owr Jewyll house there chargeing the m^r of owr Jewyls wth the same.

[36]

"And further we wyll that you charge and comande in owr name the sayd Deane there to take downe such monumentes as may geve any occasion of memorye of such supersticion and Idolatrye hereafter...."

Underneath is the following "memorandum," proving how great was the treasure possessed at that time by the authorities of the minster:—"Memorandum that by force of the above wrytten comyssyoñ there was taken owt of ye sayd Cathedrall church of Lyncoln at that tyme in gold ij^{m}vj^{c}xxj oz (2621 oz.), in sylver iiij^{m}ij^{c}iiij^{xx}.v oz (4285 oz.); Besyde a greate nombre of Pearles & preciouse stones wych were of greate valewe, as Dyamondes, Saphires Rubyes, turkyes, Carbuncles etc. There were at that tyme twoe shrynes in the sayd Cath. churche; the one of pure gold called St Hughes Shryne standinge on the backe syde of the highe aulter neare unto Dalysons tombe, the other called St John of Dalderby his shryne was of pure sylver standinge in ye south ende of the greate crosse Ile not farre from the dore where ye gallyley courte ys used to be kepte."

Harry Lytherland was the last treasurer of Lincoln. As he saw the last of the treasures carried away, he cried "ceasing the Treasure, so ceaseth the office of the Treasurer," and flinging down the keys on the pavement of the choir, he walked out of the church. This occurred on the 6th June 1540; Lytherland never sat in his stall again. Of the risings in 1536, resulting from the religious changes, Lincoln was one of the chief centres. The Lincolnshire insurgents, assembled at Horncastle, sent six demands to the king, the last being that Bishop Longland should be deprived. The Chancellor of Lincoln was captured and conveyed to Horncastle, where he was killed, and his garments and money were distributed among the rebels. The Abbot of Barlings rode into Lincoln with his canons in full armour. A number of insurgents gathered in the city, and the bishop's palace was attacked and plundered. The rebel council was sitting in the chapter-house when the messenger arrived from the king. His answer was characteristic; he reproved them for "their presumptuous follie and rebellious attempt," called the shire "one of the most brute and beastly of the whole realm," and summoned the people to depart quietly to their homes. An attempt on the part of the gentlemen to read the letter secretly caused a panic [37]among the commons, who decided to kill them all. The gentry hurriedly escaped into the chancellor's house, where they barricaded the door. Shortly after, the commons, deserted by their leaders, and "each mistrusting other, who should be noted the greater meddler, suddenlie ... began to shrinke, and got them home to their houses without longer abode" (Holinshed's "Chronicles "). On the arrival of a royal force, the cathedral was "turned into an arsenal, fortified and garrisoned." Lord Hussey, a prominent Lincolnshire noble, was executed, and the Abbot of Barlings was hanged, together with the Abbots of Whalley, Woburn, and Sawley. Another event which occurred towards the end of the same reign should not pass unnoticed. Anne Askew was a member of an old Lincolnshire family, being the daughter of Sir William Askew or Ayscough; her birthplace was probably Stallingborough, near Grimsby. "When she was at Lincoln," we are told, "she was seen daily in the Cathedral reading her Bible, and engaging the clergy in discussions on the meaning of particular texts." Her bold opinions at last brought her to the stake in 1546, at the age of twenty-five, a martyr to the doctrines of the Reformation.

A few possessions of value appear to have survived the reign of Henry, but these were sacrificed to the rapacious greed of the unscrupulous ministers of his son and successor. The following statement occurs in "An Historical Account of the Antiquities in the Cathedral Church of St. Mary, Lincoln," published in that city in 1771:—"A second Plunder was committed in this Church Anno 1548, during the Presidence of Bishop Holbech, who being a zealous Reformist, gave up all the remaining Treasure which Henry had thought proper to leave behind; this Bishop together with George Henage Dean of Lincoln, pulled down and defaced most of the beautiful Tombs in this Church; and broke all the Figures of the Saints round about this Building; and pulled down those [of] our Saviour, the Virgin, and the Crucifix; so that at the End of the Year 1548, there was scarcely a whole Figure or Tomb remaining." Henry Holbeach became Bishop of Lincoln in the year of Henry VIII.'s death, and soon after that event he surrendered to the Crown twenty-six (or according to Strype thirty-four) rich manors belonging to the see. He died at Nettleham in 1551.

[38]
Passing on to the beginning of the next century, a fire which broke out in the year 1609 partly destroyed the old library over the east walk of the cloisters; little further damage appears to have been done.

The turbulent times of the Civil War were disastrous for Lincoln in common with so many other places. An account of the troubles which the struggle brought upon the city is given by Mr. Edward Peacock in the thirty-eighth volume of the *Archæological Journal*. The shire appears to have been distinctly Puritan, and up to July 1643, at any rate, the city was in the hands of the Parliamentarians. John Vicars, the author of "Jehovah Jerah. God in the Mount or England's Parliamentarie Chronicle," printed in London in the year 1644, gives an account of an unsuccessful attempt of the Royalists to capture the city about that time. "And as proeme and preamble to the ensuing tragedie or treacherie, Serjeant Major Purfrey had let into the town, at a back gate, about sixty bloodie cavaliers, all of them disguised in countrie marketmen's habits, who were all hid and sheltred (as it was credibly enformed) in the Deane's house in Lincolne." The attempt was unsuccessful, but the city soon after fell into the Royalists' hands, an event of unhappy interest for our subject, as it gave rise to an attack (in April of the following year) of the Parliamentarians under the Earl of Manchester. The capture of the city was soon followed by the mutilation of its most glorious monument. Through the misguided zeal of the rude soldiers of the Parliament, the stained glass of the minster was nearly all broken, the tombs were injured, and the brasses torn from their matrices. It should yet be remembered that considerable damage had already been done under Henry VIII., and even earlier, and that the injuries of 1644 were not so great as it might appear at first sight. Lincoln was again attacked by the Royalists in 1648, when the bishop's palace was stormed and taken, and the city given over to plunder. In a description of the minster, published in 1771, the following account of the injury is given:—"Bishop Winniff had little Enjoyment of his Honor in presiding over this See; for in the Year 1645 ... he had the Mortification to see all the Brass Work of the Gravestones pulled up, the rich Brass Gates to the Choir and divers of the Chantries pulled down, [39]and every regaining Beauty defaced; and his Church made Barracks; for the prevailing Parties in that unhappy Reign, and his Episcopal Palace totally destroyed, both at Lincoln and Buckden."

During the time of the Commonwealth, the minster passed through a crisis such as it had never before experienced, and such as we may hope it will never experience again. "Certain godly ones," we are told, were "then gaping after its stone, timber, and lead," and the minster was in great danger of being demolished altogether. This fact has been recorded by the late Precentor Venables, who states that the fabric was "only rescued from threatened destruction by the civic worthy, Mr. Original Peart (Mayor in 1650 and Member of Parliament in 1654 and 1656), who represented to Cromwell that 'if the minster were down Lincoln would soon be one of the worst towns in the county.'"

Photochrom Co. Ltd., Photo.]

THE OBSERVATORY TOWER, LINCOLN CASTLE.

In 1654, on the 19th August, Evelyn visited the city. He has left to us in his Diary an interesting record of the Lincoln of the Commonwealth:—"Lincoln is an old confused town, very long, uneven, steep, and ragged, formerly full of [40]good houses, especially churches and abbeys. The minster almost comparable to that of York itself, abounding with marble pillars, and having a fair front (here was interred Queen Eleanora, the loyal and loving wife who sucked the poison out of her husband's wound); the abbot founder, with rare carving in the stone; the great bell, or Tom, as they call it. I went up the steeple, from whence is a goodly prospect all over the county. The soldiers had lately knocked off most of the brasses from the gravestones, so as few inscriptions were left; they told us that these men went in with axes and hammers, and shut themselves in, till they had rent and torn off some barge-loads of metal, not sparing even the monuments of the dead; so hellish an avarice possessed them: besides which, they exceedingly ruined the city."

At the Restoration, Robert Sanderson was rewarded for his long faithfulness to the royal house by the bishopric of Lincoln. He had been a chaplain to Charles I., who is reported to have said, "I carry my ears to hear other preachers, but I carry my conscience to hear Dr. Sanderson."

Sanderson died in 1663. Four years later, William Fuller, the antiquarian, was appointed bishop. "He bestowed very much in adorning his church," and restored many of the monuments and inscriptions.

Fuller's efforts at restoring something like order to the grievously ill-used fabric were seconded by those of Dean Honywood, who in 1674 caused the present arcade to be constructed on the north side of the cloisters, with the library above it. Sir Christopher Wren, the architect, did not take the least care to let his work harmonise with its surroundings. From the times of Fuller and Honywood to our own, there have been many whose energy has led them to undertake various works in and about the minster. Some have undoubtedly worked with mistaken zeal; but, taken as a whole, Lincoln has escaped with less injury than many others of our public monuments. In the year 1727 an attempt to remove the timber spires of the western towers, resulted in a serious riot (see p. 56), and the townspeople were only pacified by a promise that the spires should not be touched. No such disturbance occurred when they were finally removed in 1807, the excuse then being that they were very insecure, and would [41]cost much to repair. But it seems that even at this time the removal was not entirely approved of; a lament, clothed in ridiculous rhyme, was published in the *Gentleman's Magazine* of January 1808, and a local writer two years later relates how the "lofty spires" were "levelled by tasteless inconsiderate improvers." Early in the 18th century the western towers began to shew signs of instability, and caused considerable anxiety. An architect named John James was employed about 1730 to strengthen the towers by constructing arches underneath, which formed a kind of triple porch just inside the church. The materials of the chapel of the old bishop's palace were employed in the construction of these arches. The central porch was reconstructed by James Essex about thirty years later. An anonymous historian of about forty years ago quotes the following extract from a letter written by Sympson, at one time clerk of the works to the fabric, to Browne Willis:—"Before I make an end of this long letter, I must acquaint you that I took down the antient image of St. Hugh, which is about 6 foot high, and stood upon the summit of a stone pinnacle at the south corner of the west front, in the month of June last (*i.e.* 1743), and pulled down 22 foot of the pinnacle itself, which was ready to tumble into ruins, the shell being but 6 in. thick, and the ribs so much decayed, especially on the east side, that it declined visibly that way.... I hope to see the saint fixed upon a firmer basis before winter." The date of this work coincides with that of the appointment of Bishop Thomas (1743-61), who appears to have zealously applied himself to the repair of the fabric. The historian of 1771 writes as follows:—"During the Presidence of Bishop Thomas, and towards the first of the present Bishop Dr. Green, over this See, this Church was repaired and modernised in the State which it is this Day seen. Also, during the Presidence of Bishop Thomas, he set on Foot the appropriating the tenth of the Fines arising from the renewal of the Leases of their respective Estates, as a Fund for the continual Repair of this Church, himself setting the Laudable Example."

The "scraping process" to which the exterior of the minster was subjected under the late John Chessel Buckler of Oxford is within the memory of many. It caused much angry discussion and bitterness at the time, and resulted in [42]the publication of a book, in which Buckler undertook to justify his work on the minster. The chief part of this volume consists in long chapters of abuse, written with a most extraordinary flow of language, and directed against all who ventured to object to the way in which his work had been done.

Under the late consulting architect to the chapter, J. L. Pearson, R.A., many necessary strengthenings and restorations were carried out; but as no radical changes are in progress they do not call for detailed notice in this place.

Photochrom Co. Ltd., Photo.]

THE STONE BOW IN THE HIGH STREET.

[43]

CHAPTER II
THE EXTERIOR

The external beauty of Lincoln Minster is rendered doubly impressive by the dignity of its position. While so many of our cathedrals are at a disadvantage in this respect, the site at Lincoln, as at Durham and Ely, was most happily chosen. Had it been less exposed, the spires would probably have yet been standing, but these are a small loss compared with the advantages gained. Especially when glowing with the rays of the setting sun, the three noble towers, each a conspicuous object for miles around, create an impression not soon forgotten. The distant view of the minster has inspired the enthusiastic utterances of many writers; but it may be enough for us to describe it in the words of one of the most eminent among them. "Throughout a vast district around the city," says *Freeman*, "the one great feature of the landscape is the mighty minster, which, almost like that of Laon, crowns the edge of the ridge, rising, with a steepness well-nigh unknown in the streets of English towns, above the lower city and the plain at its feet. Next in importance to the minster is the castle, which, marred as it is by modern changes, still crowns the height as no unworthy yoke-fellow of its ecclesiastical neighbour. The proud polygonal keep of the fortress still groups well with the soaring towers, the sharp-pointed gables, the long continuous line of roof, of the church of Remigius and Saint Hugh."

Such words need no comment; it only remains to point out the positions from which the minster is seen at its best. The view from the opposite side of the river, in a south-easterly direction, is good. The long straight line of roof is broken by the bold projection of the transepts; the faultiness of the west front is not apparent, and the grouping of the three towers with their numerous pinnacles appears to advantage.

[44]

The view from Brayford, too, is fine, although in this case the foreground is perhaps not so picturesque as it might be. From nowhere does the minster look more imposing than from the towers of the castle; a water-colour by Frederick Mackenzie (see p. 53), painted from the roof of "Cobb Hall," admirably illustrates this. For a closer prospect, the best position is undoubtedly the north-east corner, especially when the sun is setting behind the western towers. Lastly, the view from the High Street, beyond the Stonebow, should not be forgotten.

The minster is built of Lincoln stone, a hard limestone, well capable of resisting the action of the weather. It yet remains to be proved whether the fast-increasing number of tall smoking chimneys will have the undesired effect of blackening the exterior and destroying the sharpness of its lines.

[45]

Photochrom Co. Ltd., Photo.]

THE WEST FRONT.

The **West Front** is massive and imposing, and possesses some features of considerable interest; beyond this, little can be said for it, as it is architecturally somewhat of a sham. Why the architects threw away the opportunities they had, and finished off the western end of the church with an enormous screen wall, it is now difficult to say. The Norman front was originally furnished with three gables, one in the centre, following the line of the old nave roof, the others in front of the Norman towers, and similar to those which may still be seen on the outer sides of these towers. The greater height of the Gothic nave necessitated the raising of the central gable, and this was done; but instead of preserving the

gables in front of the towers and adding two more for the side chapels, a huge flat wall was constructed, masking the lower parts of the towers, and altogether hiding the western chapels. The result is that the towers appear too close together, and lose all connection with the façade, which should rather set off their proportions than conceal them. There seems, too, no reason for the great width of the façade, until one passes round and sees the low side-chapels hidden behind it. Turning, however, to details, there are points which are deserving of close attention. The severe and strong wall in the centre, with a fragment of the first bay behind it, is the only part which now remains of the first Cathedral of Lincoln. In gazing on this massive work, so fortress-like and forbidding, we are reminded of the warrior-bishop [46]
[47]who first chose this spot for his cathedral, making it so solid and strong, that it was at one time seized and fortified, under circumstances already related (p. 11). The great central recess has been heightened several feet, but the two side-recesses and the lofty semi-circular niches beyond remain almost as Remigius left them. It is probable that the plainness of this bishop's work was originally relieved by colouring. The slits in the jambs of the great arches and on the front serve to light the passages and chambers, which are constructed in all directions within the thick walls of this part of the façade. The original use of these chambers cannot very well be determined; they are accessible only from the inside of the minster, and may be reached from the sills of the great west windows. There is a great difference in style between the features of this wall and those of the three elaborate doorways with which it is pierced. They are assigned to Bishop Alexander the Magnificent, and have been called by Sir G. G. Scott "truly exquisite specimens of the latest and most refined period of Romanesque, just before its transition into the Pointed style." The central doorway has four columns on either side, carved with diaper ornament and grotesque figures; elaborate mouldings are carried round the arch. The side doorways are of similar style, but with three columns instead of four to support the arches. Some of the ornament was restored between thirty and forty years ago by the architect, J. C. Buckler of Oxford, partly to take the place of the plain pillars inserted by Essex a century before, and partly to replace decayed work. The arcade of intersecting arches along the top of the Norman front is also assigned to Bishop Alexander. It has been pointed out that this bishop's work may be distinguished from that of Remigius by its being *fine-jointed*, whilst the other is *wide-jointed*. A most interesting, though perplexing, band of sculpture runs horizontally across the front; it commences just above the side niches, and is continued in the jambs of the great arches. It is most probable that the sculptures originally formed a consecutive pictorial illustration of many of the chief incidents recorded in the Old and New Testaments, but they are in no order now, and there is no doubt that they have at some time or another been rearranged—or rather disarranged. The rarity of such work as this greatly increases the importance of these Lincoln sculptures. They have been considered by [48]some to be of Saxon origin, and either to have belonged to the earlier church of St. Mary Magdalene, which stood on this spot, or to have been brought by Remigius from Dorchester. They do not, however, appear from their style to be earlier than the eleventh century, and since Remigius would have most probably arranged them differently, had they been specially sculptured for their present position, it is possible that they were inserted later than his time. That they were there not very long after, is proved by the fact that one relief on the south side of the southern tower is now enclosed in the Early English chapel, which we know to have been built before the middle of the thirteenth century, The sculptures are illustrated in the *Archæological Journal*, vol. xxv., from photographs procured when the repair of the west front was going on. The subjects were at the same time identified by Archdeacon Trollope (afterwards Bishop of Nottingham). The band is about 3 ft. 6 in. in depth, and is protected by a plain cornice. The traces of paint still seen on some of the reliefs would lead to the conclusion that the whole series was once bright with glowing colours. Parts of the original reliefs are now represented by modern copies.

Commencing over the northern niche, the first subject is the Torments of the Lost, who are seen in the clutches of demons; next is Christ standing at the jaws of hell, on the prostrate form of Satan. On the northern jamb of the recess are two more reliefs, one representing six saints, the other identified by Trollope as "Christ the Custodian of all faithful souls." Our Saviour is seated on a throne, holding a sheet before Him, in which are the souls of four personages; the symbols of the Evangelists appear at the corners. Opposite to these are two other reliefs; one represents Christ sitting at meat with the two disciples at Emmaus, the table at which the three figures are seated being placed beneath an arcade capped by turrets with conical roofs. This relief is in very good preservation, and the architectural features furnish a guide to the date of the series. The next subject is the Blessed End of the Righteous and the Torments of the Lost. On the front of the pier is a fragment of a draped figure. The next relief should be the first of the series; it represents Adam and Eve expelled from Paradise, and is placed on the southern jamb of the central recess. On the front of the pier are two |49| |50|

|51|men tilling the ground, probably typifying the Condemnation of Man to Labour, while the hand grasping a bag above would symbolise God's providing care for His people; along the top is a band of foliage. There are two reliefs on the jambs of the southern recess; the first is mutilated and obscure, but is probably intended for Hannah with the Infant Samuel, and Samuel announcing God's revelation to Eli, On the other side of the recess is Christ instructing a disciple, probably either Nicodemus or Peter. The three other reliefs, over the southern niche, are:—(1) The Building of the Ark: Noah is seen with a hammer, and another figure, probably one of his sons, with an axe, the ark being visible behind; (2) Daniel in the Lions' Den, this subject made conspicuous by a moulding all round it; (3) The Entry into, and Departure from, the Ark: to the left the ark is seen, with Noah, his wife, and three sons (?) inside, while a procession of animals in miniature is advancing towards the vessel; to the right of this are eight figures leaving the ark, with the Almighty Father beyond, apparently making the covenant with Noah. The last relief, hidden by the chapel at the south-west corner, represents the Deluge: three half-submerged figures are clinging to trees or rocks; the prow of the ark is seen to the left.

S. B. Bolas & Co., Photo.]

CARVED WORK OF THE CENTRAL DOORWAY AT THE WEST END.

The Gothic arcading which covers the later portions of the façade varies considerably in detail; this is particularly noticeable on the north and south ends, where narrow lancet doors in deep porches give access to the western chapels. These porches were at one time walled up. They are not shewn in Hollar's plate in Dugdale's "*Monasticon*," nor in Wild's or Coney's plates of 1819. The chapels are lighted by the circular windows above the doors. It has been considered by some that the Gothic part of the façade is of different periods, and that St. Hugh commenced building here at the same time as at the eastern end of the church. Others have thought that the first idea was to do away with the old front altogether, in which case the enlargement would not have commenced until later. At any rate, we may be fairly sure that the Gothic portions were all constructed some time during the first half of the thirteenth century. We can get a little nearer than this with regard to the gable in the middle and the arch beneath it, where the trellis ornament is supposed to mark the work of Bishop Grosseteste (1235-53). This bishop appears to have |52|removed the central Norman arch, and to have carried the recess up to its present height, piercing the head with the cinquefoil window, outlined by a band of finely-carved scroll foliage. Rickman calls attention to the "exquisite workmanship" of the mouldings of this window. The rest of the arch is filled with trellis-work, quatrefoils, trefoils and circles, while at the crown there is a large carved boss. In the spandrels are two niches with royal statues. The gable contains seven arches below, two of them pierced with windows. The two at the ends contain statues, and in the centre is a fragment of a carved subject. Above is another arch, over which are two angels with heads bent downwards. One of the Sloane MSS. in the British Museum contains certain "Observations" by Dr. Edward Brown in 1662. Speaking of the west front at Lincoln, the writer says that "almost at the top are four or five fine pictures, but broken down in the late troubles, but with small dexterity and by as bad a handicraft." The vast façade is finished off at the ends by two octagonal stair-turrets, capped by tall, pyramidal roofs. On the top of the southern turret is Bishop St. Hugh, with staff and mitre; on the other is the Swineherd of Stow, whose reputed gift of a peck of silver pennies towards the building of the minster has secured for his statue a position as exalted as that of the great bishop himself. The first statue is the original one, though it was once taken down and afterwards refixed on a firmer basis (see p. 41). The other is a copy of the original Swineherd, now preserved in the cloisters. The suggestion that this statue represents Bishop Bloet, the horn having reference to the bishop's name ("blow it"), is hardly worthy of serious attention. The row of canopies above the central door contains eleven royal statues, ranging from William the Conqueror to Edward III., the sovereign on the throne when the figures were placed there by Treasurer John de Welburne (d. 1380); they are all bearded, very similar to one another, and of the tamest possible character. They were originally coloured and gilt. There was a great outcry in the last century at the report that they had been removed to make room for a list of the subscribers to the iron railings which until quite recently enclosed the minster front. The following is a memorandum of Dr. Stukeley's, found in his copy of Browne Willis's "Cathedrals," when sold in 1766:—"In the beginning of 1753, the wicked chanter, Dr. [53] [54]

[55]Trimnell, of his own authority pulled down the eleven fine images of kings over the door of Lincoln Cathedral, to put up a foolish inscription of the names of the subscribers to the new iron rails." It is unlikely, however, that the statues were ever removed.

F. G. M. Beaumont, Photo.]

THE MINSTER FROM THE CASTLE.
(From a Water-colour Painting by Frederick Mackenzie, in the South Kensington Museum.)

The tracery of the great windows in the three recesses may be considered to date from the end of the fourteenth century. The three massive oak doors are studded with iron bolts and carved with Perpendicular tracery. The two statues of bishops, one on either side of the great central recess, are evidently restored. In 1796, in the *Vetusta Monumeuta*, the statues are described as "lately put up, and had been in some other place before." They must have replaced earlier figures, since old engravings shew these places to have been occupied by statues. The parapet along the top of the façade belongs to the fourteenth century, and is similar to that along the south side of the nave.

It is worthy of mention that some critics have not been so severe on this façade as others. Setting aside absurd comparisons of the last century, the late Sir G. G. Scott has stated that it always struck him as being very impressive. From behind the parapet the two fine western **towers** look out of keeping. The gables on the west faces, by which the towers were originally connected with the old front, are now hidden from view, but three rows of Norman arcading of the time of Bishop Alexander (1123-48) still project above the parapet. The details of the arcading differ in the two towers, and it will be noticed that the octagonal turrets at the corners were carried higher in the southern tower than in the northern. They seem to have remained as left by Alexander (most probably with pyramidal roofs) for two centuries and a half; Perpendicular storeys were then added to them. On each side of these upper storeys are two lofty windows, of which the lower parts are now walled up. The octagonal turrets at the corners were continued to the tops of the towers: they are crowned by wooden pinnacles, coated with lead, which are not nearly so graceful in appearance as those on the central tower, partly owing to the coating of dark paint with which they are covered. In the northern, or St. Mary's, tower was placed the original "Great Tom of Lincoln," as well as its successor, until removed in 1834, to be recast a larger size and hung in the [56]central tower. The southern, or St. Hugh's, tower, has a ring of eight **bells**. It is not known when, or by whom, the ring was formed, but the tower must have been used for bells very anciently. Until recently four of the bells were dated 1702, and the others 1593, 1606, 1717 and 1834; one was recast in 1895. The fifth bell is rung daily at morning and evening; at six in the morning, from Lady Day to Michaelmas, and at seven for the rest of the year; in the evening it is rung at eight all the year round. The day of the month is tolled after each ringing. These towers, as well as the central one, were originally crowned with tall spires of timber, coated with lead. The central spire had been blown down in a gale nearly two hundred years before it was decided by the cathedral body to remove those on the west towers, the excuse being that they had fallen into disrepair. The work of destruction was commenced on the 20th September 1726 or 1727. As the citizens in the town below saw the workmen engaged in this way, cries of indignation were raised, and towards evening a crowd of 500 men assembled to prevent the removal of the spires. The main gates of the minster yard were secured against them, but the small postern on the south side was apparently forgotten. To this the besiegers turned their attention, and, rushing up the "Grecian" stairs, they soon battered down the gate, and entered the close. One of the "Old Vicars," named Cunnington, appears to have suffered especially at their hands, whether he was the chief culprit or not. He is said to have been dragged from his house in the Vicars' Court, and compelled to dance on the minster green in the midst of the mob. The crowd only dispersed on the promise that the spires should be allowed to remain. The next day, the Mayor and Aldermen were requested by the minster authorities to send the bellman round the city with the following message:—"Whereas there has been a tumult, for these two days past, about pulling down the two west spires of the church, this is to give notice to the people of the city, that there is a stop put to it, and that the spires shall be repaired again with all speed"; "after which," we are told, "the mob with one accord gave a great shout, and said, 'God bless the King.'" The spires remained during the lifetime of these zealous townsmen, but their descendants seem either to have been more indifferent in the matter, or else to have been wanting in a similar courage, when the spires were finally [57]removed in 1807. A foolhardy feat was performed in the year 1739 by a man named Robert Cadman, who "did fly from one of the spires of the minster, by means of a rope, down to the Castle Hill, near to the Black Boy public-house." Cadman met his death in the next year at Shrewsbury, while attempting a similar performance there.

On passing round to the south side of the minster, the artificial nature of the west front becomes plainly apparent. We now get a much clearer idea of what the Norman towers were originally like. The gable, with its intersecting Norman arcades and diaper-work, is doubtless similar to that originally on the western face. In front of the towers is St. Hugh's or the ringers' chapel, with its single window to the south. Next is the chapel used as the Consistory Court, with two windows facing south, and two others facing east. The gable of this chapel is worthy of notice. At the head of its tall central lancet is a grotesque figure, commonly pointed out as the "Devil looking over Lincoln"; there appears to be no satisfactory solution of the origin of this phrase. The most curious legend is that which describes the devil as *still inside* the minster, and afraid to come out for fear of being blown away! At the heads of the the two side windows are sculptured figures which have been considered to represent pilgrims. The seven bays of the nave are indicated by stout buttresses with triangular heads carried up clear above the parapet of the aisle, over the roof of which flying buttresses are thrown. The clerestory windows are divided into groups of three, and the two windows in each bay of the aisle are separated by a slender buttress. The wavy parapet over the clerestory is of the fourteenth century, and above it stand six canopied niches for statues, with grotesque figures projecting from their bases. The cornice below has been restored at the eastern end, shewing the heads and bosses with which it appears to have been decorated for its entire length. The lofty panelled buttresses of the western side of the great transept are surmounted by tall pinnacles with niches. These pinnacles are of later date than the transept. A grotesque figure projects from each corner of their slender crocketed roofs.

At the south-west corner of this transept is the **Galilee Porch**. It will be remembered that the same name is also borne by two other celebrated porches in England, at Ely and [58]Durham. Both of these are, however, at the western end of their respective churches. The origin of the name "Galilee" has had so many different explanations, that it would be tedious to give them here, but the name may have some reference to the room above the porch, in which the judicial Court of the Dean and Chapter was formerly held. The Galilee at Durham was built for women, who were not allowed to use the church. The porch at Lincoln was constructed about the year 1230, as a state entrance for the bishop, whose palace lay on the south side of the minster yard. The plan is in the form of a cross, and the porch may be entered at the south and west ends, both of which are open. An arcade of slender arches runs round the walls. At the end of the north limb the arches are open, and rest upon a low wall.

Photochrom Co. Ltd., Photo.]

GALILEE PORCH, AND SOUTH SIDE OF THE NAVE.

The two stone coffin-covers in the pavement do not appear to have been originally placed here; they apparently date from the twelfth or thirteenth century. The porch has a stone vault, with a profusion of tooth ornament on the groins and elsewhere. Someone has left it on record that there are 5355 [59]dog-tooth pyramids used in the decoration of the Galilee Porch alone. Two massive oak doors at the east end open into the transept; the doorway is richly carved with foliage and tooth ornament. In an engraving of the year 1672 this fine porch is shewn as walled up; it was used, in the last century, as a work-shop for the plumbers of the cathedral. The ground round the minster has been considerably lowered in recent years, and in this way the proportions of the building are displayed to greater advantage. In Wild's plan of 1819, a flight of steps is indicated by which the Galilee Porch was entered, but the lowering of the ground has caused their removal. Above this porch is the room in which the **Chapter Archives** are carefully preserved. An account of these is given by the Rev. Prebendary Wickenden in the thirty-eighth volume of the *Archæological Journal.* The cathedral plumbers seem to have been accommodated here after the porch below was reopened, until the year 1851, when the chamber was appropriated as the muniment room. For nearly a century before this the documents had been kept in what is now the singing-school over the vestry. The plan of the room is **T**-shaped, and it is lighted by eleven lancet windows rising from the floor; the walls are covered with Early English arcading. The documents have suffered considerably from damp and neglect, and some of them still bear traces of the time when George Huddleston, a priest-vicar in the early part of the seventeenth century, kept pigeons in the muniment room. The two most precious documents are now preserved in the cathedral library; one of the few existing contemporary copies of the Magna Charta, and a copy, made early in the twelfth century, of the Charter of William the Conqueror for the transference of the see from Dorchester to Lincoln. A charter from Edward I., of the year 1285, is also still preserved, by which permission is given to build walls round the close, and to shut the gates of the same at night. Lastly may be mentioned a series of Chapter Acts, nearly complete from 1305 to the present time, and audit accounts covering the same period.

The embattled parapet which surrounds the low modern roof is in the Perpendicular style, and is, of course, later than the structure itself.

Photochrom Co. Ltd. Photo.]

THE CENTRAL TOWER, FROM THE SOUTH.

From a point a little westward of the Galilee Porch, the **Central Tower** is seen to advantage. Its early name of the [60]"Rood Tower," from the rood-screen which fills the easternmost of the four great interior arches supporting it, has been corrupted into "Broad Tower." Very excellent authority could be brought forward for calling this the finest central tower of any English cathedral. The height to the top of the corner pinnacles is 271 feet, an altitude which is exceeded by only two cathedral *spires* in England, those of Salisbury and Norwich. The tall spire of timber, covered with lead, which originally crowned this tower reached an altitude, it is said, of 525 feet; but this is doubtful. This spire was blown down during a tempest in January 1547-8. The outside measurement of the sides of the tower is 54 ft. 6 in. This is not the first central tower of Lincoln. The original tower, of Norman work, was succeeded by a *nova turris,* which fell about the year 1237. The celebrated Grosseteste was bishop at the time, and the work of reconstruction would appear to have been begun almost immediately. The lower part of the present tower, both inside and out, bears the peculiar lattice-work ornament which has been noticed in the gable of the west front. Here, as there, it may be considered [61]a mark of Grosseteste's time. The tower was then carried as high as the top of the arcading just over the ridge of the nave roof, and a wooden spire was added. In this state it appears to have remained for at least half-a-century. When the work was again taken in hand, in 1307, it was speedily completed, and by 1311 the tower was raised as high as we now see it. The two lofty windows which occupy each side of the upper storey, with their crocketed pillars and canopied heads, are extremely beautiful. At the four corners are octagonal panelled turrets, surmounted by wooden pinnacles coated with lead. The spire which fell in 1547-8 carried the parapet with it. In February 1715 three of the pinnacles were blown down; their re-erection was completed in 1728. Nearly fifty years later, the dean wrote to James Essex, the architect, asking his opinion about the erection of a stone spire. He replied that the height was too great and the situation too exposed, but recommended, instead, battlements and four stone pinnacles. In 1775, Essex was employed to erect the present open parapet. The western side was blown down in December 1883, but, falling inwards, it did little damage, and was easily replaced. The following details concerning the tower are copied from a pocket-guide to Lincolnshire by the late Sir Charles Anderson, Bart, (third edition, revised by Canon Maddison), a most interesting book containing much useful information:—"It was a bold undertaking, and executed with marvellous skill, for, in order to lessen the additional weight without building strengthening arches below, which would have injured the interior effect, as at Salisbury and Wells, two thin walls are tied together at intervals, so as to leave a vacuum between, bound by squinches at the top corners.... Compared with the great Victoria Tower of Westminster, which, from many points of view, looks broader at the top than the bottom, the Lincoln tower is the perfection of symmetrical proportion; the reason is that it is gathered in about 2-½ inches, 25 feet below the parapet, which shews upon what trifles, as they might be called, beauty and proportion depend." Wallcott describes this tower as "so full of state, and dignity, and majestic grandeur, that no church in England, or on the continent, can be cited in the same description."

Bells in the Central Tower.—The tower is the abiding-place [62]of the present "Great Tom of Lincoln"; but before describing him and his companions, we must give an account of his predecessors of the same name in the north-west tower, as well as of the former occupants of his present abode. We find that in 1311 a question arose respecting new ropes for the two bells lately hung in the new tower. These were not the first bells possessed by the minster, as there is a record in the works of Giraldus Cambrensis of "*duas campanas grandas atque sonoras*" given by Geoffrey Plantagenet, who held the temporalities of the see from 1173 to 1182. The number was afterwards increased to six, although it is not known when. They were called the "Lady Bells," and were rung for the minster service. The largest Lady Bell was tolled forty times at the shutting of the church doors every night, after which the searchers of the church partook of bread and beer provided for them under the watching chamber in the east transept; they then walked round and searched the church. When the Lady Bells were taken down in 1834, four were found to be dated 1593, one 1633, and one 1737. The original "Great Tom" was hung in the north-west tower. It is not known how it was acquired; some say it was a gift, others say it was stolen from the Abbey of Beauchief, Derbyshire, or from Peterborough. The origin of its name, too, has been a subject of dispute. Stukeley considered it possible that it had been consecrated to St. Thomas of Canterbury. Others think it took its name from that of the old bell of Christ Church, Oxford, which bore the curious inscription, *In Thomae laude, resono Bim Bom sine fraude*. It should be remembered that Oxford was in the diocese of Lincoln in olden days, and that several Bishops of Lincoln were chancellors of Oxford. Wherever the first "Great Tom" came from, it was recast in the minster yard by two bell founders from Nottingham and Leicester early in the seventeenth century, when the weight was increased from 8743 pounds to 9894-½ pounds. "The bell was cast and hung upp and upon Sonday the xxvij of this month [January 1611] ronge owte and all safe and well." It was tolled until 1802, when it was found that this process shook the tower too much. The following extract from the *Stamford Mercury* of the 6th August 1802, is given by North in his "Church Bells of Lincolnshire":— "Great Tom o' Lincoln is to be rung no more! The full swing of four tons and a half is found to [63]injure the tower where he hangs. He has therefore been chained and rivetted down; so that instead of the full mouthful he has been used to send forth, he is enjoined in future merely to wag his tongue." Towards the end of the year 1827 [64]experienced ears detected that something was wrong, and by Christmas it became plainly evident that the bell was cracked. It was finally decided to have it recast in a larger size. For this purpose it was broken to pieces with its own clapper, and sent to London. To provide the extra metal, the six Lady Bells were unfortunately sacrificed. The cathedral thus lost the distinction of being the only one in the kingdom possessed of two rings of bells. "Great Tom" was recast by Thomas Hears at the Whitechapel Bell foundry on the 15th November 1834. It was taken by road to Lincoln, drawn by eight horses, and raised to its new position in the central tower. Two new quarter bells, cast at the same time, were also hung in this tower. The number of quarter bells was increased in 1880 to four, one new bell being given by Mr. Nathaniel Clayton, and the other by Mrs. Seely, The present "Great Tom" weighs 5 tons 8 cwts., is 6 ft. 0-¾ in. high, with a circumference at the base of 21 ft. 6 in., and is in size the fourth bell in the kingdom. The hours are struck upon it with a hammer weighing 224 lbs.

F. G. M. Beaumont, Photo.]

THE MINSTER FROM THE CLOISTERS.
(From a Water-colour Painting by Frederick Mackenzie, in the South Kensington Museum.)

The chief feature of the south side of the western transept is the beautiful round window, "the bishop's eye," with its delicate leaf-like tracery. From the outside, this window would look much better if it were a little higher up, but the reason of its position is sufficiently evident from the inside, where it is quite clear of the vault, while the admirable round window on the north side is spoilt by not being completely visible until you approach it very closely. Above "the bishop's eye" is a horizontal band of seven elaborately-carved quatrefoils, considered to have formed part of the tracery of the earlier round window. They are enough to shew that the window was different to "the dean's eye" at the other end of the transept. The window in the gable, though much too large for its position, is nevertheless worthy of notice on account of its fine flowing tracery, which was inserted, like that of the round window below, about the middle of the fourteenth century. This window is not visible from the inside. The gable is outlined by a curious band of open Gothic tracery, surmounted by a cross. This band was erected by the architect to the fabric, named Hayward, in the year 1804. It is a copy of the original (see old view, p. 21), constructed about the time of the insertion [65]of the window below. This was blown down on the 20th January 1802. It fell at about eleven o'clock in the morning, but fortunately did little damage. It will be noticed that the two turrets are different: the western is octagonal and crocketed; the other is shorter, plainer, and four-sided. Near the top of the last buttress on the east side of the transept is a stone with the date 1746, apparently a record of restoration. The roof of the choir of St. Hugh, the earliest Gothic portion of the building, is somewhat lower than that of the nave; the clerestory windows are remarkably slender. The narrow buttresses are later additions, constructed to resist the thrust of the stone vault. In the corner of the east transept is a small stone flue from the old fireplace in the choristers' vestry. At the south-west corner of this transept is the canons' vestry; the buttresses, which appear above, pass right down to the ground, and are seen inside the vestry, clearly shewing this to be a later addition to the transept. Over this vestry is the room where the muniments of the chapter were kept until they were removed to the chamber above the Galilee Porch. The room they had occupied was then appropriated as a singing-school, and a small organ was erected in it, which is still there. The vestry is plain and unpretending, but it would have been a pity if, as was at one time proposed, it had been altogether removed. In 1854 it was thoroughly restored under the architect, J. T. Willson, when the present parapet was added. Underneath are seen the low windows of an old vaulted crypt, which was probably used as a treasury. The south face of the slender transept of St. Hugh looks very different to that of the western transept; its many windows leave but little wall space. First is a pair of lancets, then two rows of three above them, and lastly three narrow lights to fill the gable. On either side are two octagonal turrets, with pyramidal roofs surmounted by sculptured figures of angels. On the east side of the transept are seen the two semi-circular chapels of St. Hugh's design. On the buttress at the south-eastern corner of the transept are two sundials, with inscriptions, one being the familiar quotation from Martial—*Pereunt et imputantur*, the other is *Cito ætas præterit*.

The **Presbytery**, or eastern limb of the minster, is the finest example of the best period of English Gothic. [66]Its crocketed gables and pinnacles, its panelled buttresses, its elaborate tracery, and, above all, its wealth of sculpture, form a striking contrast to the simplicity of St. Hugh's work. The choir is divided into five bays, indicated by the boldly-projecting buttresses, once covered with statues; the canopies and pedestals still remain, within arches supported by tall clustered pillars with foliaged capitals. The buttresses are crowned by slender crocketed gables, at the bases of which grotesque figures project. One of these, an imp on the back of a witch (on the third buttress), serves, like the sculpture in the gable of the consistory court, for the "devil looking over Lincoln."

Photochrom Co. Ltd., Photo.]

SOUTH-EAST PORCH, WITH THE CHANTRY-CHAPELS OF BISHOPS LONGLAND AND RUSSELL.

F. G. M. Beaumont, Photo.]

CAST OF THE FIGURE OF CHRIST, IN THE SOUTH-EAST PORCH.
(Taken before the Porch was restored.)

Both in the aisles and in the clerestory, broad windows, filled with elegant geometric tracery, take the place of the plain lancets seen in other parts. The most magnificent exterior feature of the eastern arm is undoubtedly the sculptured doorway on the south side. Leland, in the time of Henry VIII., writes: "There is a very faire Doore in the [67]upper part of the Churche Southward to go into the Close, and againe this lyith the Byshop's Palace hangginge *in declivio*." It was probably constructed, like the Galilee doorway, as a state entrance for the bishop. The porch fills the third bay, and projects as far as the buttresses; its sides recede inwards to the pair of doors giving access to the Angel Choir. Although the doorways of our cathedrals, as a rule, cannot in any way be compared with the magnificent portals to be seen in France, yet this single example at Lincoln would be quite enough to prove that English architects were capable of designing a really magnificent doorway. In the tympanum is the subject of the Last Judgment in relief. A majestic figure of Christ the Judge occupies the central space, with an angel on either side swinging a censer. He is surrounded by a quatrefoiled [68]aureole supported by angels. To the left, the dead are rising from their tombs, and are borne aloft by angels; on the other side demons are dragging the condemned down to the jaws of hell, which gape wide open beneath the Saviour's feet. The archivolt is richly decorated with sculpture. In the inner band is a row of niches with twelve seated figures, apparently kings and queens: next a double band of delicate open-work foliage; outside this a row of sixteen slender standing figures enclosed by interlacing stems, richly decorated with foliage. The doorway is formed of two cinquefoiled arches, separated by a central pillar having the canopy and base for a figure of the Virgin, which has been removed. On either side of the doorway is a triple canopy for statues, and behind this a row of slender columns with foliated capitals.

The hand of the restorer might well have spared this beautiful porch, where the question of the stability of the fabric did not in any way arise. But, unfortunately, an attempt was made about thirty years ago to restore the mutilated figures, and further restorations are now [1897] being carried out. A cast of the headless figure of Christ, with the two angels at the sides, has recently been acquired by the South Kensington Museum. It is valuable as shewing the state of the central figure before restoration (see illustration, p. 67). It is believed that Essex also had tampered with this door in the last century. On the buttresses on either side of the doorway are four headless statues, resting on corbels supported by projecting figures.

The two small **chapels** which stand to the right and left of the doorway are those built as chantries by Bishops Russell and Longland. The one on the eastern side is that of Bishop Russell (d. 1494). The mullions which run from top to bottom of the three windows, dividing them into vertical strips, are sufficient to mark this building as of the Perpendicular period. Between the windows there is only just room for the panelled buttresses which separate them. The embattled parapet, far more conspicuous and elaborate than one of an earlier period would have been, is covered with tracery, and broken by crocketed pinnacles. The whole shews on a small scale the extravagance into which Gothic architecture had lapsed, and contrasts unfavourably with the sober dignity of the structure to which this small chapel is attached. The other chapel to the west was built half-a-century later by Bishop Longland (d. 1547). [69] [70]

[71]Although an imitation of Bishop Russell's, it shews points of difference both inside and outside. Leaving these chapels, we notice on the second buttress from the east a queenly figure. On the eastern buttress is a statue of Edward I., trampling on a Saracen, and by his side is his Queen, Eleanor of Castile, whose effigy is to be seen inside this choir.

Photocrom Co. Ltd., Photo.]

VIEW FROM THE SOUTH-EAST.

The **east end**, in spite of its defects, is perhaps the finest in the country, and the broad expanse of the minster green offers exceptional opportunities for seeing this part of the building to advantage. An excellent general view may be had from the south-east, in the direction of Pottergate. The main feature is the magnificent central window in the geometrical Decorated style. Above this is another fine window of the same period. The latter looks somewhat awkward on account of its position, balanced, so to speak, on the apex of the window below; like the window over the "bishop's eye," it is far too large for the gable in which it is placed. In the trefoil over the top is a figure of the Virgin with the Infant Saviour, and on either side of the gable is a turret with a richly crocketed pyramidal roof. The aisle windows (the two which are filled with the beautiful early stained glass) look very small when compared with the giant central window, from which they are separated by panelled buttresses of bold projection. We have already noticed the insincerity of the west front of the minster, and the same charge must be brought against this eastern end, although the deception here is not so extensive. The two panelled gables over the aisle windows are shams; there is nothing behind them, and they appear to have been only designed for the sake of effect. The northern gable is higher than the other, and the tracery is not quite the same. An arcade runs right across the lower part of the front, beneath the three principal windows. Another short arcade is seen beneath the sham gables.

The hexagonal stone structure at the north-east corner, with a pyramidal roof, covers the minster well. This stonework is presumably not very ancient; in a view of Hollar's in Dugdale's "*Monasticon Anglicanum*," the well is covered by a wooden shed.

On the north side of the angel choir, the second bay contains the chantry chapel of Bishop Fleming (d. Jan. [72|1430-1), which formed a model for the two chapels on the other side of the choir. The parapet is panelled, and the buttresses contain niches for small statues. In the next bay is a door leading into the choir; its position corresponds to the sculptured porch on the other side, but it is much smaller and plainer. One of the mouldings of the arch is of oak; in the tympanum is an aureole with a bracket for a figure. The doorway is divided by a central shaft, an addition of the latter part of the fourteenth century. The shield of arms in front of the capital is that of Richard II. (1377-99); quarterly, first and fourth, the mythical Arms of Edward the Confessor; second and third, the Royal Arms of England. The supporters are—dexter, a lion; sinister, a bull. It will be noticed that the next window of the aisle, and the buttress beyond it, are much plainer than the rest, left so doubtless owing to their having been to a great extent hidden by the walls of the lengthened chapel (see p. 20).

In the year 1875 the ground round the chapter-house was lowered, and the foundations of the chapel were laid bare. They extend as far as the second buttress of the angel choir. A general idea of the appearance of this chapel may be had from a view of Hollar's, in Dugdale's "*Monasticon*." There were two windows in the east wall, and above

28

these a blind arcade. The roof was pointed; its outline may still be traced on the transept wall.

Between this chapel and the vestibule of the chapter-house is the old common chamber, of which parts are now used as a lavatory. The position of the ten-sided chapter-house, like that of the neighbouring cloisters, is somewhat unusual. Two windows, with a lozenge-shaped panel above them, occupy each of the sides. The buttresses attached to the walls at the angles were originally crowned by pedimental gables, all but the two westernmost of which have been replaced by crocketed pinnacles of the Decorated period. The pressure of the stone vault, which was added some time after the chapter-house was built, necessitated the strengthening of the walls, which was done by means of flying buttresses attached to eight huge blocks of masonry, standing about 20 feet from the walls. The roof is pyramidal, and is surmounted by a cross. A guide-book of 1810 states that there was "originally a fine spire rising from the roof, but was taken down not [73]long since, being greatly decayed." This apparently refers to an alteration made by James Essex in 1761-2, when the roof was "reduced to an ugly hipped shape." It was again altered to its original form in the year 1800. A wall, which is shewn in early prints, between some of the outer buttresses was removed in 1806. On several of the buttresses the marks may still be seen of houses once built against them. These houses have now been all removed, and a delightful view of the minster has been obtained by clearing away all the dwellings which stood until quite recent years on the now vacant piece of ground beyond the chapter-house.

H. C. Oakden, Photo.]

NORTH DOORWAY OF THE ANGEL CHOIR.

The north side of the minster is, to a large extent, blocked by the deanery, but a fine general view may be had [74]from the road at the north-east corner, with the chapter-house just in front, surrounded by its massive supporters. The transept of St. Hugh, beyond this, is hidden by the chapter-house vestibule and the cloisters. At the end of the western transept is the circular window, the "dean's eye," with the large quatrefoil in the middle, surrounded by a band of sixteen small circles. Above, in the gable, is a lancet window of five lights. The difference between these two windows and those inserted in a corresponding position on the south side of the transept, is very noticeable. The southern pair are over a century later in date. Both the turrets on the north side are octagonal, but neither of them is crocketed. The view from this spot at sunset is particularly fine. After passing the deanery, and turning to the left, it will be noticed that the north side of the nave has not a row of niches such as has been seen on the south side. The tower at the west end has a gable on its north face, similar to that on the opposite side of the companion tower.

A visit to the minster would not be complete without a climb to the breezy top of the great central tower. The ascent is not difficult, and may be made for a small fee. The clock was made by William Potts & Sons of Leeds, in 1880, and weighs about four tons. It took the place of one made in 1775 by Thwaites, and afterwards improved by Vulliamy.

The Cathedral Close, or **Minster Yard**, as old-fashioned Lincoln people still love to call it, was first protected by a wall in the last years of the thirteenth century. The licence from Edward I. to the Dean and Chapter, giving them permission to undertake this work, dates from the year 1285. Edward's successor granted a further licence in the year 1319 to fortify the walls; the two ruined towers in the chancery garden are relics of the fortifications begun about this time. Massive double gateways were erected to protect the approaches, except in one instance, where a steep ascent was considered to justify the erection of a single gateway only. Unfortunately, these gateways were for the most part destroyed early in the present century. The principal one remaining is that opposite the western end of the minster, known as the "Exchequer Gate." Indeed, even when all the gateways were standing, this seems to have been the chief.

S. B. Bolas & Co., Photo.]

NORTH SIDE OF THE ANGEL CHOIR.

Leland, who was at Lincoln in the latter part of Henry [75]VIII.'s reign, writes thus: "Al the hole Close is environid withe an highe stronge wawle havynge dyvers Gats in it, whereof the principall is the Escheker gate." Of course, when Leland wrote, the companion outer gateway was yet standing, and it remained so until early in the present century. It had [76]then fallen into disrepair, and does not seem to have been considered worth renovating. An idea of the appearance of the Exchequer Gate will be gained from De Wint's picture, reproduced on p. 33. Like its former companion, it has a large archway in the middle and a postern on either side; above are two storeys of rooms, formerly let as dwellings. A guide-book of the year 1810 mentions that a public-house was at that time "kept in the apartment to the north of the southern postern." Another gateway of the same period (early fourteenth century) is still standing near the top of the New Road, at the south-east corner of the close. This was the only single gateway. It is now called "Pottergate Arch." A little westward of this gate, a flight of steps, with a postern at the top, leads up to the minster yard from the New Road. Respecting its name, the "Grecian Stairs," much has been written. It may be sufficient here to remark that the old name appears to have been simply "The Greesen," from the early English *gree*, a step.

"a sentence
Which, as a grize or step may help these lovers."

("Othello," Act I. sc. iii.).

The "Priory Gate" to the north-east, near the chapter-house, is a plain modern arch, a poor substitute for the two gateways destroyed in the year 1815. In addition to those already mentioned, there were anciently two other double gateways to the close. One of them stood between the White Hart and Angel Inns, at the west end of Eastgate; the other was near the deanery, at the end of East Bight.

The venerable ruins of the old **Palace of the Bishops** at Lincoln bear sufficient testimony to long years of neglect. But it is gratifying to know that this beautiful spot has been restored in recent years to its ancient use, and that a new bishop's palace now occupies an appropriate place beside the ruins of the old. It lies on the south side of the close, and anciently commanded a lovely view over the straggling city in the valley beneath, and over the surrounding country. The prospect is now marred by a fast-increasing number of tall, smoking chimneys, signs of awakening activity; but it is still beautiful, and the view of the minster from the palace grounds is as fine as ever.

[77]

ELEVATION OF THE FORMER CHAPEL OF THE BISHOP'S PALACE, WITH BISHOP ALNWICK'S TOWER.

[COMPLETED FROM BUCK'S PRINT, 1726.

[78]

Special permission is necessary to visit the ruins. The entrance gateway, at the corner of the Vicars' Close, bears the arms of Bishop Smyth. The chapel used to stand on the left, where the coach-house and stable now are. In front is Bishop Alnwick's tower, which was restored by the late bishop, Dr. Wordsworth. Just westward of the tower are the ruins of the hall, extending in a southerly direction towards the ruins of the kitchen. The present chapel of the bishops stands between the ancient hall and kitchen, and has been quite recently erected. There are also remains of buildings of less importance.

The Deanery lies on the north side of the minster, just beyond the cloisters. The present house, built half-a-century ago, replaced a much finer building, with a quadrangular central court. The commencement of the old deanery is dated as far back as the end of the twelfth century, but the chief part was the work of Dean Fleming (1451-83). Leland seems to imply that there were traces of more ancient buildings. "Where the Deane of Lyncolnes Howse is," he says, "and there about was a Monasterye of Nunes afore the time that Remigius began the new Mynstar of Lyncolne: and in this Howse yet remayne certayne tokens of it." The demolition, towards the end of the year 1847, of the fine tower built by Dean Fleming caused much regret. It used to be called "Wolsey's tower," from the popular opinion that it was built by that celebrated prelate when bishop of Lincoln. In the painting by Mackenzie, reproduced on p. 53, the tower is shown, to the left of the chapter-house. The new deanery lies a little to the eastward of its predecessor.

The most interesting of all the old houses around the minster yard is the **Cantelupe chantry house**, which stands almost opposite to the south-east doorway of the minster, near the entrance to the Vicars' Court. This house was originally the residence of the clergy who served at the altar of St. Nicholas in the minster, where Nicholas, Lord Cantelupe, founded a chantry in the year 1355, with an endowment for the maintenance of three priests. It is probable that the house was erected by Lord Cantelupe's widow eleven years later, when the foundation was enlarged by her for a warden and seven chaplains. The house is of stone, with a fine oriel window, which has, however,[79]been much mutilated. The two shields of arms, one on either side of this window, are those of the Cantelupe and Zouche families. In the gable above is a niche, with a seated figure of Christ. Several windows of the house [80]have been filled in, and the interior has been completely transformed.

PLAN OF THE BISHOP'S PALACE, LINCOLN, ON THE LEVEL OF THE HALL FLOOR.

VIEW OF THE ANCIENT DEANERY.

Close by is the entrance to the **Vicars' Court**, founded by Bishop Oliver Sutton (1280-99); the work was continued by his successor, John de Dalderby, and taken up again by Bishop John Buckingham (1363-1397), The entrance gateway is the work of Bishop Buckingham, and bears his shield of arms. Some houses on the east side of the court also bear these arms, and date from the same bishop's time. Part of Bishop Button's work is to be traced in a house on the south side. The other buildings are of later date. The residence of the chancellor, on the eastern side of the close, near the south end, may be recognised by its fine old red-brick front, dating from the latter part of the fifteenth century; parts of the house are of earlier date. The precentory stands on the south side of the close, next to the Exchequer Gate. Very little now remains of the ancient building; the present front was designed by J. L. Pearson, R.A. The next house eastward, the sub-deanery, has more extensive remains of early work; a bay window of [81]the fifteenth century should in particular be noticed. In the year 1884, when the eighteenth century railings at the western end of the minster were removed, and the ground round this part lowered, the sub-deanery was considerably altered to allow of the widening of the road.

PART OF THE ANCIENT DEANERY, WITH DEAN FLEMING'S TOWER.
[82]

CHAPTER III
THE INTERIOR, INCLUDING THE CLOISTERS AND CHAPTER-HOUSE

A detailed description of the interior of Lincoln minster may be fittingly preceded by a brief review of its chief features. As regards the Presbytery or Angel Choir, no one, with the exception of a recent American critic, has ventured to lower the just reputation of this lovely work, distinguished for a rare combination of beauty of architecture and sculpture. The next place in point of architectural excellence must be assigned to the Nave, a harmonious and characteristic example of the Early English style. But the unique position the choir of St. Hugh holds in the history of Gothic architecture should not be lost sight of. The principal interior defect, and this rendered all the more conspicuous by the general gracefulness of other parts, is the lowness of the vault. But, after all, there are only four loftier vaults in England, and one of these is only higher by two feet; nevertheless the defect is conspicuous, and is a serious one. Of the windows, the most noticeable are the great east window and the two "eyes," and these are equal to any in their respective styles in the country. The modern coloured glass which fills the former, as well as many lesser windows in the minster, brings out in greater contrast the loveliness of even the wrecks of the early stained glass still remaining in some others.

Considering that Lincoln once possessed the monuments of a queen, of another direct ancestress of our Royal family, and of two bishops whose fame has spread to the farthest limits of Christendom, as well as of others of more local celebrity, it must be confessed that the monuments at present in the minster are disappointing. That of Queen Eleanor is represented by a modern reproduction; Catherine Swynford's is mutilated almost beyond recognition; those of St. Hugh and [83]Grosseteste are gone altogether; and the ancient monuments which are left retain very little of their original splendour.

The **Ground Plan** illustrates the lengthening process to which the building has been subjected. It is a double cross, with side chapels extended beyond the nave walls at the western end. The lesser transept has four apsidal chapels towards the east, and the great transept has a single eastern aisle divided into six chapels. The symmetry of the presbytery has been disturbed by the addition of projecting chantry-chapels, one on the north side and two on the south. The cloisters are accessible from the eastern transept, and the chapter-house from the cloisters.

The westernmost bay of the nave has been formed into a kind of **vestibule** by means of the archways constructed, during the last century, to strengthen the towers at that end. The vestibule is in three compartments, two of which, under the western towers, are square. The centre one is the most interesting, since it preserves to us a portion of the first bay of Remigius' nave. High up in the side walls is a Norman arch, part of the original clerestory. Below this we can trace the outline of a wider arch (now filled in), which belonged to the triforium. Considerable alterations were made in these walls by Treasurer Welburne in the second half of the fourteenth century, and the arches were filled in during the early part of the eighteenth century, owing to the instability of the towers. The arch dividing the vestibule from the nave was constructed by an architect named John James (apparently not James Gibbs, as some have supposed) about the year 1730, and altered by James Essex thirty or forty years later. In the time of Bishop Grosseteste (1235-53) the side walls were carried above the Norman clerestory to the height of the present nave, and covered with the characteristic lattice-ornament which we have already seen in the central arch outside. The great west window was also inserted in Grosseteste's time, as well as the cinquefoil window above. The tracery now filling the former is in the Early Perpendicular style, and dates from the end of the fourteenth century. From the broad sill of this window a good view of the interior can be obtained, and a much finer one still from the passage which runs beneath the other window above. From the latter position we have an uninterrupted view of the entire length of the minster, which [84]looks longer than it really is, from the fact that the vaulting is carried at an almost uniform height throughout.

ELEVATION OF ONE BAY ON THE NORTH SIDE OF THE NAVE.

In the floor are slabs bearing the names of Chancellor Reynolds (d. 1766) and of Precentor Trimnell (d. 1756), the "chanter" who was accused of removing the statues over the central doorway outside. On the wall at the north-east corner is a tablet to the memory of the officers, non-commissioned officers, and privates of the 10th or North Lincolnshire regiment of infantry, who died in the campaigns of the Sutlej (1845-46) and of the Panjab (1848-49); the tablet was erected by their surviving comrades. The compartments under the western towers were vaulted by Treasurer Welburne (ab. 1350-80), to whom is also due the tracery which covers the walls. The curious chambers constructed in the thickness of the old Norman west front are accessible from the sills of the western windows, these being joined by narrow passages in the wall. On the north side we are able in the same way to reach a long narrow chamber, which probably served as a treasury, constructed in the north wall of the tower. The chamber was originally lighted by four small round-headed windows. One of them, on the west side, is still open; the two facing northwards, formerly outside windows, are now enclosed by the northwest chapel, and blocked up; the fourth, on the east, is also blocked. A square hole in the floor formed at one time the only means of access to the chamber beneath, which may now be reached by a doorway [85]from the porch. In the north wall of this lower chamber is a low semi-circular arch, supposed to have been constructed by the Norman builders, in order to avoid some obstacle in the way of the foundations. This arch was filled in with masonry, now pierced by a doorway. The north-west chapel, which is entered by this doorway, encloses the outer wall of St. Mary's tower.

HALF SECTION OF THE NAVE, LOOKING WEST.

The corresponding chapel on the south side of the minster is sometimes called the "Ringers' Chapel." On its walls is painted a seventeenth century list of the "Names of the Companie of Ringers of our Blessed Virgen Marie of Lincolne." In one place we see "Edward Whipp 1617 at the kings coming to Lincolne." This refers to the visit of King James I. in March of that year, when he visited the minster, and touched a number of persons for the evil. His Majesty went also to a cock-fight at an inn near the Stone-bow, and to a horse-race on the Heath. Edward Whipp was evidently one of those who rang the bells in honour of the royal visit. The Ringers' Chapel encloses part of the south wall of St. Hugh's tower, which has a large arched recess and a niche, similar to those in the west front.

The curious "stone beam," about which so much has [86]been conjectured, and so little is known, is constructed between the walls of the two western towers, just above the stone vault of the nave. It is really an arch of very slight curvature, composed of twenty-three stones of unequal length, but of uniform depth and breadth. Examination has proved that there is nothing but mortar in the joints, and there are no traces of iron having been used in the construction. When jumped upon, the "beam" vibrates appreciably. It has been suggested that it was constructed in order to try whether the towers were capable of supporting the additional weight of upper storeys, but nothing appears to be satisfactorily known as to the purpose it served or the date of its erection.

The **Nave** was constructed, together with the two chapels at its western end, during the first half of the thirteenth century. Attempts have been made to distinguish earlier and later features in different parts. For example, the morning chapel on the north side is considered to be somewhat earlier than the consistory court opposite to it; but there being no documentary evidence to guide us, all that we may safely say is, that the nave is later than the time of St. Hugh (d. 1200), and was practically completed before the death of Bishop Grosseteste, which occurred in 1253. Taken as a whole, it is one of the best examples of the Early English style we possess. The late Sir G. G. Scott, in his lectures on Mediæval Architecture, thus speaks of it—"It exhibits an Early English style in its highest stage of development: massive without heaviness, rich in detail without exuberance, its parts symmetrically proportioned and carefully studied throughout, the foliated carving bold and effective, there seems no deficiency in any way to deteriorate from its merits." In dignity especially, the eminent architect considered the nave to be superior to all other parts of the cathedral.

Photochrom Co. Ltd., Photo.]

THE NAVE, LOOKING WEST.

The general complaint against the interior—the lowness of the vault—is applicable here. The architects were, undoubtedly, influenced by the vault of St. Hugh's choir, which is 8 feet lower than that of the nave. According to the measurements in Lord Grimthorpe's "Book on Building," the height is 82 feet—21 feet less than is found at Westminster, 11 feet less than at York, 6 feet less than at Ripon, and 2 feet less than at Salisbury. Lincoln comes fifth of the English cathedrals in interior height, but since this height is maintained almost uniformly [87]throughout, the vault looks lower than it really is. For this reason the defect is not so noticeable in looking westward from beneath the great tower. Another complaint, which appears hardly so justifiable, is the remarkable lightness of the piers, and the great width of the arches. Many, in fact, might be inclined to agree with Mr. F. C. Penrose, who points out that the effect of this lightness is an increase in the dignity and apparent size [88]of the nave, which would be felt to a much greater extent if the windows had their original stained glass, and thus admitted less light than at present. Mr. Penrose has investigated the matter, and given the result in the Lincoln volume (1848) of the Archæological Institute. He states that "the ratio of voids to solids appears to be more remarkable than is to be found in any vaulted building in Europe; at least, among the larger structures." The piers, we are told, are quite secure. The greatest care was taken in their foundations, and the footing courses extend so as to reach those of the side walls. The nave is in seven bays, the two westernmost of which are conspicuously narrower than the others. The reduction is a little more than 5 feet, the measurements being 26.6 feet, and 21.3 feet.

Another peculiarity, already noticed, is that these two western bays are not quite in a straight line with the others (see p. 23). The vault drops about 2 feet, and turns slightly northwards. Each pier of the nave is surrounded by eight circular shafts, some more slender than the others; the slender ones are separately banded in the middle. The shafts are principally of Purbeck marble, which is capable of receiving a fine polish. This marble has been used extensively throughout the interior. It has, however, become much decayed, and in many parts has had to be renewed; whilst in some cases it appears to have been replaced by the far more durable Lincoln stone. Many of the Purbeck shafts in the minster are being polished up or restored. The bases of the nave piers are seen to be higher on the north side than on the south. This peculiarity is also found in the western transept, in St. Hugh's choir, and in the Angel Choir beyond. The "dean's eye," too, on the north, is higher than the round window at the southern end of the transept, and on the west front of the minster, the lower rows of arcading on the north side are at a higher level than the corresponding rows on the south. It has been conjectured that this peculiarity was owing to the inequality of the ground. If it had been a mere freak of St. Hugh's architect, it seems, hardly probable that the succeeding architects would have imitated it for another century. Turning again to the nave, a difference will be noticed in the foliage of the capitals on the two sides. The arch mouldings, like those of St. Hugh's choir, were considered "beautiful specimens" by Rickman. They are deeply cut, and throw good, bold shadows. [89]In the triforium, each bay contains two arches, supported by clustered columns with foliaged capitals. The spandrels are decorated with sunk trefoils or quatrefoils. In most cases the arches are each divided into three sub-arches with clustered shafts, the tympanum being pierced with quatrefoils. A difference is noticeable, however, in the easternmost arch, and the two westernmost bays (five arches altogether) on both sides. Here the sub-arches are only two in number. [90]The narrowness of the two western bays accounts for the variation at that end. The clerestory is the same throughout its length, having three tall narrow windows in each bay, with slender banded shafts. In the nave we have, according to Fergusson, "a type of the first perfected form of English vaulting." He calls it "very simple and beautiful." At the junctions of the ribs are elaborate bosses of foliage. The compartments are covered with plaster, once decorated in colours and gold. In the second bay from the east is the name: W. L. PARIS:—evidently intended as a record of some repairs to the vault. The springers rest on clusters of three long slender vaulting-shafts, rising from foliaged corbels just above the capitals of the nave piers.

S. B. Bolas & Co., Photo.]

PART OF THE DOUBLE ARCADING OF ST. HUGH.

In the aisles, each bay has two lancet windows, except the easternmost bay on the south side, which has only one. In the jambs are slender Purbeck shafts, twice banded. Just beneath these windows, an arcade of trefoiled arches runs along the whole length of the nave, being continued on the screen walls to the western chapels. The arches are deep, with bold mouldings, and are supported by clustered columns. There are five arches in each bay, but they are not placed in the same manner on both sides of the nave. On the south, the arches are arranged in groups of five, with blank spaces of wall between, in front of which pass the vaulting-shafts. On the north, the arcade is continuous, and is so arranged that each cluster of shafts supporting the vault passes in front of an arch. The work on the south side is more elaborate; tooth ornament is used, a string-course runs along at the height of the capitals, and foliaged bosses are found in the lower corners of the spandrels. In addition to the clustered vaulting-shafts already mentioned, there is a single vaulting-shaft in the centre of each bay, between the windows, rising from a corbel above the wall-arcade. On the north side these corbels merely have plain mouldings, but on the south side they are foliated. The arrangement of the vaulting-ribs is different in the north and south aisles; and in the latter it will be noticed that some of the bosses have figure-subjects, besides the foliage met with on the north side. The *Agnus Dei* carved on the boss in the fourth bay from the west should be noticed. To such minor differences, continually found in the corresponding parts of a Gothic edifice, the style undoubtedly owes a peculiar charm. In the case of the nave at Lincoln, they [91]probably indicate a slight difference in the date of erection, but they certainly point to a far greater scope for individuality being accorded to the masons than was allowed in the rigidly symmetrical styles of the Renaissance. The chapel at the south-west corner of the nave is used as the Consistory Court, and that opposite to it was reappropriated to its ancient use as the Morning-Prayer Chapel by the late Archbishop Benson, when Chancellor of Lincoln. A small brass tablet to his memory has recently been fixed to the wall by the side of the altar. Both chapels are stone-vaulted, but the northern has a feature which is not found in the Consistory Court. This is the slender Purbeck column in the centre, erected to support the vaulting. In this chapel was formerly placed the massive font of black basalt, which was removed in 1874 to its original position in the second bay from the west on the opposite side of the nave. The font is of Norman workmanship, and apparently dates from the time of Remigius (1067-92). There is another of a similar character in the cathedral at Winchester. The basin is square, and rests on a massive circular drum in the centre and four small columns at the corners, supported by a square base. Round the sides of the basin, a row of grotesque monsters, some winged, is carved in bas-relief. The font is now raised on steps. It was used by the parishioners of St. Mary Magdalene's, whose church was destroyed to make room for the minster. They were allowed to worship in the nave until the time of Bishop John de Dalderby (1300-20), when a new church was built for them. The old pavement of the nave was removed towards the end of the last century (about 1782), when many of the grave-slabs it contained were taken away. 8 It was in the nave that the gorgeous processions of olden days were formed, and the original pavement was marked with two rows of circles to indicate the different positions of the clergy. The pavement of the north aisle is considered by some to have been slightly raised; from it the populace might then have watched these processions. Of English cathedrals, Lincoln comes next to Canterbury for the richness of its stained glass, but there is little in the nave which is worthy of notice. Almost all that escaped the stray arrows and bolts from the bows of dwellers round the close appears to have been destroyed [92]during the disastrous times of the Civil War in the seventeenth century, when the mere beauty of a work of art appears to have often served as a sufficient excuse for its destruction. In the windows of the aisles the glass is all coloured, but modern. The lower lights of the great west window are also filled with modern glass, the work of two amateurs, the Revs. Augustus and Frederick Sutton, who produced many others of the coloured glass windows in the minster; the upper lights contain fragments of glass of the same date as the tracery (latter part of the fourteenth century). The cinquefoil window above has been filled with modern glass, inserted in 1859 in honour of the founder, Remigius, who is seen in the centre, holding his church in one hand, and his bishop's staff in the other. The windows of the clerestory are plain.

The nave has very few monuments. Of those which remain, the foremost place must certainly be taken by the dark mutilated slab under the easternmost arch on the north side. Remigius, it will be remembered, was originally buried near the altar of the Holy Cross, where his tomb-slab was broken by the beams which fell in flames from the roof of the Norman church. Some years ago, a monumental slab, in two parts, with carved subjects, which might very well date back to the time of Remigius, was brought to light in the cloisters. Canon Massingberd had this removed to the spot where it now lies, not far from the original burial-place of the bishop. The carving consists of various scriptural subjects in low relief; it is now much worn. The surrounding inscription records the foundation of the cathedral by Remigius in the year 1072, and the restitution of the tomb-slab in 1872. On the opposite side, at the end of the aisle wall, is a marble tablet in memory of Michael Honywood (b. 1597: d. 1681), who was made Dean of Lincoln in the year of the Restoration. The present library was erected by him at a cost of £780, and received his collection of books.

Near the western end of the nave are slabs in the floor, marking the burial-places of Bishops Smyth (d. Jan. 1513-14), Alnwick (d. 1449), and Atwater (d. Feb. 1520-1). Bishop Smyth was the founder of Brasenose College, Oxford. Bishop Alnwick was buried in the place where he used to stand when processions were formed in the nave. Besides the slabs in the pavement, other monuments of a more conspicuous [93]character appear to have once adorned the nave. A century ago, beneath the easternmost arch on the south side there stood "a raised Altar Tomb of grey marble, this for Dean Mackworth; it was once very costly adorned with figures of Brass Work, but defaced in the time of Cromwell." No altar-tomb now recalls the memory of the dean who refused to walk in a straight line in processions, and brought armed men into the chapter-house to lend weight to his arguments.

The carved mahogany **Pulpit** against the second pillar from the east on the north side has been moved to its present position from the choir. It may be hardly necessary to remark that the idea held by some, that this pulpit dates from the time of James I., is quite erroneous; the slightest examination will shew that very little, if any, could be of so early a period. The details of the ornament are of the last century. It is hexagonal, and is supported on open arches of ogee form. A sounding board has recently been suspended above. The brass eagle lectern was given as a memorial of the late Dean Butler (d. 1894), whose recumbent effigy now rests in the angel choir. Before passing under the central tower, an irregularity at the western end should be noticed. The great arch which spans the nave, separating it from the vestibule, is not placed in the centre; it will be seen that there is more wall space on the south side than on the north.

The **Central Tower** rests on four lofty arches supported by massive piers. These piers were enlarged to carry the additional weight of the upper storeys of the tower, and are surrounded by banded shafts, chiefly of Purbeck marble. The foliage at the crown of each arch should be noticed; the same occurs on the great central arch of the west front. Above the spandrels, which are covered with the trellis-work also seen elsewhere, are two rows of arcading, with slender clustered shafts. There is a passage all round the upper arcade, and the wall behind is pierced with four windows on each side. The vaulting, like that of the western towers, was erected by Treasurer Welburne (d. 1380); it is 125 feet high. The iron rings in the great piers, two or three feet from the ground, were used for fastening the ropes of the Lady Bells, which were hung in the tower above, and were rung before service by the four choristers in black.

[94]

The **Western Transept** is considered to be the least satisfactory part of the interior of the minster. The lowness of the vault is especially noticeable. In fact, it had to be raised in the last bay to the north, in order to include the whole of the circular window, part of which would otherwise have been cut off. Yet the transept possesses features of considerable interest. It was planned and commenced by St. Hugh and continued by his immediate successors. A low aisle runs along the eastern side, divided into six chapels, which are dedicated respectively (beginning at the north end) to St. Nicholas, St. Denis, St. James (or St. Thomas), St. Edward the Martyr, St. John the Evangelist and St. Giles. To the walls of these chapels we must look in order to trace the limit of St. Hugh's labours. A characteristic of the bishop's work is the curious double arcading on the walls he built (see p. 89). It is found in the choir and the eastern transept. Mr. Parker's theory that the front arcade was an afterthought, put up when the original flimsy walls were strengthened to support the vault, has been already given in his own words (p. 18). To whatever circumstance the feature may be due, its effect is certainly very good. It will be noticed that the two chapels nearest the choir, and parts of the two chapels next to them, have this double arcading, in which a slight difference has been pointed out. On the north side, the trefoiled arch is against the wall, and the simple arch in front; on the other side the order is reversed. This fact seems rather to strengthen the opinion of those who consider the double arcade to have been designed as such from the beginning. The end of this arcading must be taken to mark the limit of St. Hugh's work. An arcade of single arches is seen in the last chapel on each side, and this simpler design is continued round the other walls of the transept, the arches varying in breadth and resting on clustered shafts. The chapels each occupy one bay of the aisle, and are formed by projecting "perpeyn" walls of stone, originally continued to the piers by wooden screens. The arcading of these walls is deserving of attention. It now remains to notice the screens placed between the piers, to separate the chapels from the transept. The most interesting is that of the chapel nearest the choir on the south side, sometimes called the "Works Chantry." The endowment of this chapel was to provide for prayers on behalf of the benefactors of the church, both living and dead. The screen is of carved [95]stone; round the arch is the inscription "Oremus p*ro* be*ne*factorib*us* istius Ecclesie" in Gothic characters. On each side are two small kneeling figures, representing the chaplains who served the chantry. Above is a canopy with a seated figure of a bishop and the Royal Arms of England. The shield of arms is a help in assigning a date to the screen. It contains the *fleurs-de-lys* as assumed by Edward III. in the year 1338, when he laid claim to the French crown. The screen was probably erected soon after this date. It could not have been much later, since Henry IV., towards the end of his reign, reduced the number of *fleurs-de-lys* to three, in imitation of the French king, Charles V. The corresponding chapel on the other side has a feeble imitation of this screen in pine-wood, a work of the end of the last century. The other screens are of oak, carved with Perpendicular tracery, partly in openwork; they apparently date from the latter half of the fifteenth century. The altars are no longer standing, but in the middle chapel to the north the sockets for the pillars which supported the altar-slab may |96|still be seen. In one of the pavement-slabs in the next chapel to the south, nine holes are pointed out, which served a very different purpose. They are said to have been used for games by some of the officials (choir-boys, one would suppose) connected with the minster.

Photochrom Co. Ltd., Photo.]

THE WEST TRANSEPT, LOOKING SOUTH.

The two large round windows in the end walls are the most interesting features of this transept. That on the north, the "**Dean's Eye**," is of the same date as its surroundings, and may be placed about the year 1220. The tracery of the southern window, the "**Bishop's Eye**," is much later; it is of the Decorated period, and was probably inserted soon after the middle of the fourteenth century. It has already been remarked that the row of quatrefoils above the window *outside*, are relics of the earlier tracery. Near this window was John de Dalderby's shrine. Although this bishop's admirers could not bring forward a record of sufficiently numerous miracles to procure his canonisation at the papal court, yet he was revered as a saint by the people, and it has been suggested that the offerings at his shrine may have supplied the means to insert the tracery of this window, as well as the one above, which lights the roof, and can only be seen from the outside. The round window has been sometimes called the "Prentice's Window"; but this name is never heard now, and the two "eyes" of the minster will always retain the name which they have borne for more than six hundred years. The "dean's eye" and the "bishop's eye" are both mentioned in the "Metrical Life of St. Hugh," which, it will be remembered, was written sometime between the years 1220 and 1235. The simplest explanation of the names seems to be that the one faces the deanery and the other faces the bishop's palace, but a far more poetic interpretation than this has been devised. The north is the region of Lucifer, and in that direction the dean's eye must look to guard against his approach. Meanwhile the bishop's eye is turned towards the sunny south, the region of the Holy Spirit, whose sweet influence alone can overcome the wiles of the wicked one. Both windows are filled with fine early glass. The "dean's eye" presents a most magnificent example of early thirteenth century stained glass, earlier than most of the glass at Canterbury, which is the richest of all our cathedrals in works of this nature. The subject has been described by C. Winston in the Lincoln |97|volume (1848) of the Archæological Institute. It represents the Church on Earth and the Church in Heaven. In the centre is our Saviour seated in the midst of the Blessed in Heaven. Around are four large compartments, containing portions of different subjects, which do not appear to have all originally belonged to their present positions. The most interesting is that shewing the translation of the relics of St. Hugh, represented as borne on the shoulders of crowned and mitred personages. Of the sixteen outer circles, the topmost represents our Saviour seated on a rainbow; on either side are angels with the instruments of the Passion; in the next circles St. Peter and other saints are conducting holy persons to heaven; below these is the General Resurrection; the lowest five circles each contain the figure of an archbishop or bishop. The subjects can be best seen from the neighbouring triforium or from the passage which runs just beneath the window; it will be noticed that the glass in some of the compartments is much mutilated, as might naturally be expected, considering its antiquity. From below, the subjects are confused and not easy to distinguish, but the rich and harmonious blending of the colours can be seen to the fullest advantage, and the general effect is much finer. Rickman believes the form of the tracery to be quite unique in England, but states that there is a window exactly similar at Laon. Beneath the window is an arcade of seven lancet arches; the wall behind five of them is pierced with windows, which are filled with old glass, chiefly medallions and fragments. Below are two larger lancet windows, one on each side of the dean's doorway. That to the west represents angels seated amid foliage and playing musical instruments; the three lowest figures are quite distinct, but the two above are confused. These fragments have been removed from some other part of the minster, probably from the west window of the nave; they date from the end of the fourteenth century. The more easterly window is filled with old geometrical patterns and fragments. The doorway leads to the deanery, and has a porch outside. Over the door, inside, is a modern clock, with a carved wood canopy which, according to the tablet below, had been originally placed over an earlier clock in the minster. Thomas of Louth, Treasurer of Lincoln, gave a clock to the church in 1324, considered to be the one formerly at the south end of this same transept. The canopy [98]was for some years in the church at Messingham, and was removed thence to its present position, on the north side.

The "bishop's eye" on the south side is filled with delicate and beautiful flowing tracery, which has been compared to the fibres of a leaf. Rickman considers it to be the richest remaining example of its period. It is enclosed within a kind of arch formed by two rows of openwork quatrefoils; an open framework of a similar nature is often to be seen round circular windows in French cathedrals. The glass consists of fragments from other windows, chiefly of the Early English period. Although the pieces are placed quite at random, forming no subject whatever, yet the effect of the colouring is good, especially when seen from the opposite end of the transept. Of all the modern windows in the minster, with their elaborate subjects, it may safely be said that not one can be compared in effect with this mass of glowing colour. The glass in the four lancet windows below also dates from the Early English period. It chiefly consists of medallions containing various subjects, collected from other windows. The rest of the stained glass in the transept is modern. Towards the north, the ribs and bosses of the vaulting were decorated some years ago with colours and gold, in imitation of the original colouring.

The southern limb of the transept was the site of a shrine which shared with those of the two St. Hugh's the attention of the numerous pilgrims to Lincoln. In the pavement near the western wall towards the Galilee Porch is a slab with the inscription *D'Alderby Episc.* MCCCXIX. His monument is said to have consisted of an altar-tomb of "rare marble," surmounted by a rich canopy. The shrine, of "massey silver," was enriched with diamonds and rubies, and encompassed with rails of silver-gilt. It went with the other valuables to replenish the coffers of the spendthrift Henry VIII. Leland mentions that Dalderby's "Tumbe was taken away *nomine superstitionis.*" Two stone shafts belonging to the monument, and a fragment of a third, still remain against the wall. It will be remembered that it was through the energy of this bishop that the upper portion of the present central tower was erected. On the west wall, against the Galilee door, is a marble slab with a bust in relief of Dean Samuel Fuller (b. 1635: d. 1700), who received the appointment, according to Kennet, through [99]the interest of the lay lords, who loved him for his hospitality and his wit. In the southernmost chapel, on the opposite side of the transept, is an altar-tomb against the south wall. Its date is about the end of the fifteenth century, and it is probably the tomb of Sir George Talboys.

A stone screen filling the eastern tower arch separates St. Hugh's choir from the transept. The screen is a magnificent example of Decorated work, dating from about the end of the thirteenth century. It originally carried the crucifix or *rood*, which from the other end of the nave must have stood out clearly against the soft glowing colours of the great east window. On either side of the central doorway are four deep arches supported by detached pillars, decorated with grotesque heads and small figures of bishops. The wall behind is richly carved with diaper designs, shewing much freedom and variety. This screen was once decorated with colours and gilding, traces of which are still visible. It appears to have suffered a good deal at the hands of iconoclasts; many statues have doubtless been removed, and one must be very cautious with regard to the decoration which remains, as it was considerably restored by a mason named James Pink during the second half of last century.

The screen now carries the organ erected in 1826, "when also the church underwent a thorough cleaning." The organ has since been enlarged. The richly-carved case was designed in the Gothic style by the architect E. J. Willson of Lincoln. In olden days the organ filled the easternmost arch on the north side of St. Hugh's choir. Hollar's view of the year 1672, in Dugdale's "*Monasticon Anglicanum*" shews it in this place. In its present position it serves to break the long *vista*, which otherwise might be somewhat monotonous, from the extreme west end of the nave. A new organ is in course of erection at a cost of £4000; yet it seems hardly likely that instrumental music will become a prominent feature in the minster services, so long as the singing retains that high pitch of excellence which it acquired under the late Mr. Young, and maintains under his successor, Dr. Bennett. The two side doorways leading into the north and south aisles of the choir are somewhat earlier than the screen between them. They are beautiful examples of carving, dating from the end of the Early English period. The exquisite openwork foliage which runs round the arch [100] is executed with the utmost skill and care, and is without the laboured effect of so much of our later stone-work. The injured parts were carefully restored about 1770 by James Pink, who was also employed by Essex on the canopy of the reredos. The doorways have modern iron gates: it is probable that the "brass gates" carried away by the Parliamentarian soldiers used to be here. It is well worth while to notice the gorgeous effect of the early glass in the end windows of the aisles, as seen through these doorways. The soft harmony of their lovely transparent mosaic contrasts greatly with the washed-out appearance of the glass in the large window between them.

H. C. Oakden, Photo.]

[101]

AISLE DOORWAY, NORTH OF ST. HUGH'S CHOIR.

S. B. Bolas & Co., Photo.]

[102]

THE CHOIR, LOOKING EAST.

[103]
The ritual choir occupies the four bays built by St. Hugh, crosses the eastern transept, and includes two bays of the Presbytery, or Angel Choir beyond. Passing through the central doorway of the rood-screen, the choir before us is historically of the highest interest, both on account of its architecture and of its builder.

One gazes with a feeling of peculiar veneration on the walls which we know St. Hugh to have planned and reared. It is easy to imagine with what just pride and satisfaction the great bishop must have regarded these very walls, the earliest example of the pure Gothic style in this country or in any other (see p. 14). Although worthy of the closest examination, it can hardly be said that, taken as a whole, the work is beautiful; its importance is much greater from an archæological than from an artistic point of view. Certain details are of the highest excellence; but the vault, as so many have pointed out, is positively ugly, and the squat form of the great arches only serves to shew how little reliance can be placed on the outline of an arch as a guide to the date of its erection.

St. Hugh's choir is in four bays, the westernmost of which is somewhat narrower than the others. In the original piers, the central column was diamond-shaped, surrounded by eight circular shafts, which were detached, a mark of their early period. "The foliage of the capitals is exquisitely beautiful, and though distinguished technically by the name of *stiff-leaf foliage*, because there are stiff stalks to the leaves rising from the ring of the capital, the leaves themselves curl over in the most graceful manner, with a freedom and elegance not exceeded at any subsequent period. The mouldings are also as bold and as deep as possible, and there is scarcely a vestige of Norman character remaining in any part of the work" (*Rickman*).

In each bay of the triforium there are two arches, both divided into two sub-arches, with a solid tympanum pierced with a trefoil or quatrefoil. The eastern bay of the triforium on each side is of simpler design than the rest. In the clerestory, there are three windows to three bays, and two to the fourth, on each side. The fall of the central tower in 1237-9 worked great havoc in this part of the building. The vault was crushed, and the western bays were much weakened and damaged. The original slender shafts round the two westernmost piers on each side were converted into clumsy columns without capitals; this no [104]doubt added considerable strength, but rendered them far from beautiful. The arches, too, had to be partly reconstructed. In the first arch on the south side, the rings of stone across the mouldings mark the point where the later work joined the earlier, but did not quite fit. A similar example of faulty jointing will be seen on the corresponding arch on the north side towards the aisle. Turning to the triforium, we see that in the western bays clumsy eight-lobed pillars have taken the place of the original clustered shafts. These have been compared by Precentor Venables to "pounds of candles." They are certainly very ugly, and were probably intended only as a temporary makeshift. The crooked state of some of the trefoils and quatrefoils of the tympana is probably due to the same cause. The vault is most remarkable, and is fortunately unique. "The architect has made each cell strike obliquely to points dividing the central ridge of the bay into three equal parts, so that neither the cells nor the diagonal ribs from either side ever meet one another, but each cell is met by an intermediate or an oblique transverse rib from the opposite side" (*Scott*, "Lectures on Mediæval Architecture"). As this vault appears to have been constructed after the fall of the tower, we can hardly consider the deviation to be the result of inexperience, and there seems to be no excuse for this extraordinary freak. The shafts supporting the vault are alternately hexagonal and circular. They were originally carried down to the springing of the great arches, and thence continued in front of the piers to the ground. When the choir-stalls were added, these shafts were cut away to make room for them, and finished off with panelled corbels.

This part of the building, which had received such a severe shaking by the fall of the tower, was further strengthened by the erection of the arcaded screens between the piers. They fill all four arches on both sides, dividing the choir from the aisles to the north and south. The next bay eastward, which crosses the lesser transept, is filled on both sides by screens of wrought ironwork, having that scrolled pattern so often found in early examples. They are illustrated in the South Kensington Museum Handbook on Ironwork, by Mr. Starkie Gardner, who calls them the best preserved specimens of their style now existing in England. The screens are apparently thirteenth-century work, and they might be as early as the time of St. Hugh. The awkward row of gas-jets along the top is in strange [105]contrast to these fine screens. Above the latter, on each side, two constructive beams of oak stretch across the arch. One is at the height of the pier capitals, and the other on a level with the base of the triforium arcade. An attempt was made in the last century to mask their ugliness by encasing them in Gothic work of carved wood.

The magnificent series of oak **Choir-Stalls**, with their forest of pinnacles rising to the height of the pier-capitals, forms one of the chief glories of the minster. They were considered by Pugin to be the finest examples in the kingdom. Their erection, in the third quarter of the fourteenth century, is due to the munificence of the treasurer, John de Welburne, a great benefactor of the minster. A full list of the carvings was given by the late Canon Wickenden in the thirty-eighth volume of the *Archæological Journal*. The stalls are in two rows, the upper of 62 seats, and the lower of 46; the former number has now been increased by six, and the latter by two. The upper stalls have elaborate trefoiled canopies, surmounted by an intricate maze of buttresses and pinnacles, rising to a height of 24 ft. 6 in. above the choir floor. The niches above the canopies have recently been filled with statues of saints in the Anglican Calendar. The stalls in both rows are provided with hinged seats or *misereres*, intended to serve as supports in the long services during which the occupants of the stalls were required to stand. These seats, as well as the elbow-rests and finials, are richly carved with those grotesque subjects in which the mediæval artist so greatly delighted. The carver has given full scope to a most fertile imagination. Scriptural subjects do certainly occur on some of the *misereres* in the upper row, but others are of a playful character. The fox is seen preaching to birds and beasts, and then running riot among them; monkeys are at play, or occupied in the more serious business of hanging one of their number and burying him afterwards; we also find men fighting with wild animals; the labours of husbandry; kings, knights, ladies, dragons, griffins, lions, hogs, and wyverns. Whether there is a hidden meaning in any of these quaint subjects, it is perhaps difficult now to say, but the preaching fox is certainly suggestive.

To raise each *miserere* in order to examine the subject underneath would not only prove to be a somewhat tedious and dusty task, but in some cases would lead to disappointment, [106]when nothing but a plain block is seen where the carved subject ought to be. A few of the original *misereres* in the lower row are missing, and have been replaced in this way. Those who have not the time or the inclination to examine all the subjects, may take the following as representative examples of the whole series. They are all in the upper row; the lower *misereres* are, as a whole, inferior, and are restored to a much greater extent. Commencing with the precentor's stall on the north side of the door in the rood-screen, the poppy-head in front is carved with the monkey episode referred to above. The numbers in the following list are counted from the precentor's stall; the names are those inscribed on the tablets hung up at the back of the stalls. The subjects are in each case those carved underneath the *misereres*:—

(2) Archdeacon of Lincoln—a fine head and two roses.

(4) Archdeacon of Bedford—foliage.

(5) Archdeacon of Huntingdon—a man beating down acorns, and pigs feeding.

(8) Milton Manor—the gateway of a castle, and the heads of two warriors in armour.

(10) Bedford Manor—grotesque winged monsters.

(12) Welton Beck—a boy riding on the back of a bird.

(18) Welton Rivall—a mermaid with comb and mirror.

(22) Biggleswade—two men with a plough, drawn by two bullocks and two horses; to the left, a man with a harrow; to the right, sacks of corn.

(31) Carlton cum Dalby—an Ascension, with two angels swinging censers.

This is the last stall on the north side before the new ones, which were erected to cover a residence pew, in the year 1778, at the same time as the bishop's throne opposite.

Turning to the south side, and numbering from the dean's stall to the west, the following are worthy of notice:—

(1) Dean—the Resurrection of Christ.

(2) Sub-dean—a knight on horseback.

(4) Norton Epi.—the Coronation of the Virgin, and angels with musical instruments.

(9) Leicester St. Margaret's—the Adoration of the Magi.

(16) Ketton—two monkeys, one riding on a lion, and the other riding on a unicorn.

(26) Asgarby—a king enthroned under a canopy.

[107]

(28) Corringham—a lion fighting with a winged monster.

The front panels of the vicars' stalls and the choristers' desks in the lower range are carved with Gothic tracery, in the panels of which are angels with musical instruments, saints and kings.

An engraving in Wild's "Lincoln Cathedral" gives a good idea of the appearance of the choir when the old box pews were still existing. They were extremely ugly, and not only did they hide much of the fine carved work of the stalls, but their erection led in some cases to parts of the older work being cut away. Between forty and fifty years ago, when the organ was enlarged, the stalls underwent some slight repairs, and were oiled. In 1867-8 they were again strengthened and restored. The wooden tablets hung at the backs of the stalls are inscribed with the Latin titles of certain psalms. It is recorded in the "Black Book" or "Consuetudinary" of the cathedral that "It is an ancient usage of the church of Lincoln to say one mass and the whole psalter daily, on behalf of the living and deceased benefactors of the church." To ensure the complete performance of this duty, the bishop, and each member of the chapter, was made responsible for the repetition of one particular portion of the psalms. The tablets record the psalms which the occupants of the several stalls are bound to recite. At the installation of each prebendary, the dean or his representative still calls the attention of the newly-installed to the titles of the psalms hanging over his head, and reminds him of the obligation to repeat them "daily if nothing hinders." The custom is exceedingly old. A MS. in the chapter library, considered to be not later than the end of the twelfth century, gives a list of persons, with the special psalms which each should repeat. Further information on this point will be found in Canon Wickenden's article referred to above (p. 105). The usage was adopted by the late Archbishop Benson at Truro.

The **Bishop's Throne** and the **Pulpit** are modern. The former is at the east end of the stalls on the south side. It was carved in wood by Lumby, in 1778, from a design by James Essex. It has a tall Gothic canopy, with a figure of Christ holding a lamb in His arms; and is further ornamented with small carved figures of saints and angels; the panelled front is new. [108]The earlier throne, which the present one replaced, was designed by Sir Christopher Wren. The pulpit opposite is still later in date. It was erected in recognition of the services of Prebendary Trollope (afterwards Bishop of Nottingham) to the cause of architecture in the diocese of Lincoln. It was designed by the late Sir G. Gilbert Scott, and executed in 1863-4 by Messrs. Ruddle of Peterborough. The pulpit is of oak, with scriptural subjects in relief and statuettes. It has an elaborate Gothic canopy of wood, and a marble base. On the whole, it can hardly be said to be worthy of imitation. The subjects are carved with little regard to durability; some of the most delicate parts project so considerably that small portions have already been knocked off. The canopy, too, awkwardly fixed to the pillar behind, looks like a huge extinguisher, threatening to descend on the head of the preacher. In the middle of the choir is the litany desk, with the old stone beneath, inscribed with the words *Cantate hic.* The foundations of the eastern limb of Remigius' church lie beneath the floor; the semi-circular apse stretched a few feet beyond the spot where the litany desk now stands. A little way to the east is a fine brass chandelier, suspended from the vault by means of an iron rod, partly gilt. It has scrolling branches, supporting sixteen lights, and bears the date 1698. The brass lectern is of the eagle form, and was made in London, as an inscription records, in the year 1667. The following are the inscriptions it bears:—ECCLES CATHED B MARIÆ LINCOLN—DD. IOHANNES GOCHE ARMIGER AN. DOM. 1667; and above—GVLIELMVS BORROVGHES LONDINI ME FECIT 1667. The dates of these two fine specimens of brasswork suggest that they may have taken the place of earlier pieces removed by the soldiers of the Parliament.

The stone **Reredos** is enriched with Gothic arcading in the Decorated style. Parts of it belong to the latter half of the thirteenth century, but it dates principally from the time of James Essex. The original reredos was double, with a space in the middle used as a sacristy. Essex's screen was preceded by one of classical style, erected soon after the middle of the seventeenth century. It is shewn in Hollar's plate of the year 1672 in Dugdale's "*Monasticon Anglicanum.*" This screen was removed to Sleaford Church, and [109]was used in the chancel there until about fifty years ago. The tall central canopy of the present screen was designed by James Essex in the style of the monument of Bishop William of Louth (De Luda, 1290-98) in the choir of Ely Cathedral; it was carved by James Pink, in the year 1769. An altar-piece in oils formerly occupied the middle arch at the back of the canopy. It was painted and given by the Rev. William Peters, LL.B., and bears his signature, with the date 1800. The subject is the Annunciation. It is called "a beautiful picture" in a guide-book of the year 1810, but modern critics might form a somewhat different opinion; those who wish to judge for themselves may find the picture in a dusty corner of the triforium, where it is now very appropriately stowed away. The late J. C. Buckler removed the solid wall at the back of the canopy, and inserted the mullions and tracery. The first arch to the east of the lesser transept on the north side is occupied by the **Easter Sepulchre**, probably erected by someone who intended the western portion for his own tomb. It is a fine piece of stone-carving in the Decorated style, and dates from about the end of the thirteenth century. It is in the form of six slender canopies, with trefoiled arches. The three sleeping soldiers in the right-hand lower panels should be noticed. A Latin inscription was placed by Bishop Fuller on the middle one of the three left-hand panels, stating that this was the burial-place of Remigius. Of course, it is quite impossible that the bishop should have been originally buried at this spot, and it is improbable that the body was ever removed here. In Sanderson's survey is the following record:—"In the choir, on the north side, two tombs, not known. But it is famed that one of them is Remigius, whose bare sheet of lead is now (1658) to be seen. No inscription, coat, or other mention of anyone." There is some well-carved foliage on the side panels beneath the canopies.

Two mutilated tombs are now squeezed together under the corresponding arch on the south side of the choir, beneath a flat-arched canopy, dating from the second half of the seventeenth century. These tombs have been robbed of their brasses. The first is that of Catherine Swynford, daughter of Sir Payne Roet, and widow of Sir Hugh de [110]Swynford of Kettlethorpe. She afterwards became the third wife of John of Gaunt, who was made Earl of Lincoln in 1362, and was for a long time resident in the city. Henry Beaufort, son of John of Gaunt and Catherine, was bishop of Lincoln at the time of his mother's death, which occurred in 1403. The other tomb under the same canopy is that of Henry's sister, Joan Beaufort, who became the wife of Sir Robert Ferrers, and afterwards of Sir Ralph Neville, Earl of Westmorland. Before being placed as they are at present, the tombs stood side by side in this same bay. Leland, the historian of the time of Henry VIII., gives the following account of them, which shews that they cannot now be far from their original position:—"In the Southe Parte of the Presbytery lyithe in two severalle high marble Tumbes in a Chapell Catarine Swineforde the 3. Wife to John of Gaunt Duke of Lancaester, and Jane her Daughter Countes of Westmerlande." After having been robbed of all that was considered valuable by the soldiers of the Parliament, the tombs were left in a neglected condition, until at the Restoration they were placed under this arch, and the canopy was erected over them. The brasses, of which the matrices are still seen, no doubt formed part of the "bargeload" which was floated down the Witham to the sea.

The brass gas-standards behind the altar-rails were designed by J. L. Pearson, R.A.

The **South Aisle** is separated from the choir by the stone screens already mentioned. The opposite wall has a double arcade, such as we have seen in some of the chapels of the western transept. The arcading of the two westernmost screens dates from the time of Bishop Grosseteste (1235-53). That of the fourth screen is slightly later in date. The third screen is in the Decorated style, and formed a back to the famous **Shrine of the Little St. Hugh**, a boy who was said to have been crucified by the Jews in the year 1255.

It is difficult now to say whether there is any truth at all in such legends, which, it need hardly be remarked, are not confined to Lincoln, nor even to England. The story of St. William of Norwich is a similar one, and there were strong communities of Jews in both cities. As the thrifty habits of these people, often untrammelled by conscientious or humane [111]motives, caused them to grow rapidly wealthy, the hatred with which they were commonly regarded increased in corresponding measure. The Jews were not likely to get a fair hearing anywhere, and any accusations against them were readily accepted and eagerly spread. There is evidence in the poems of Chaucer that the popular prejudice was deeply rooted—

"O yonge Hugh of Lincoln, sleyn also
With cursed Iewes, as it is notable,
For it nis but a litel whyle ago." ("Prioress' Tale.")

There are several versions of the legend, one of which begins thus—

"The bonnie boys o' merrie Lincoln
Were playing at the ba',
And wi' them stude the swete Sir Hugh
The flower among them a'."

It goes on to relate how the ball strayed into the Jew's garden, into which the little Hugh was wiled, and "slicked like a swine."

Hugh is said to have been about eight years old at the time of his death. Matthew Paris mentions the legend, and says that many Jews came together to Lincoln on the occasion. They appointed a Jew as judge, to represent Pilate, and by this man's sentence the boy was afflicted with various torments before being put to death. The boy being missed, inquiries were made by his mother, and the body was at last found at the bottom of a well belonging to a Jew's house. It was given to the Canons of Lincoln, who honourably buried it as that of a martyr, in their Cathedral. According to Matthew Paris, the name of the Jew who took a leading part in the affair was Copin. He was tied to a horse's tail, dragged to Canwick

Hill, and there hanged. Many other Jews were executed as accomplices, and a large number imprisoned. Traditions say that Copin lived in one of the still remaining "Jews' houses" in the Steep. The terrible massacre of the Jews in Lincoln, Norwich, York, and other towns in the time of Richard I., was probably instigated by such tales as this.

The shrine, which remained perfect until the Civil War of the seventeenth century, was in the Decorated style. The base still remains, and on it has been placed a fragment of the original canopy. The arcade behind, of five arches, is carved with the [112]ball-flower, a distinctive mark of the period; traces of colouring and gilding still remain. The stone coffin below was opened in the year 1791, when it was found to contain the skeleton of a child, 3 ft. 3 in. long, encased in lead.

An inscription in the pavement of the aisle marks the burial place of Henry of Huntingdon (b. between 1080 and 1085: d. about 1155). This famous chronicler, who has recorded many interesting facts concerning the history of Lincoln, was probably brought up in the household of Bishop Bloet. In 1109 or the following year he was made Archdeacon of Huntingdon (then in the diocese of Lincoln). It was at the request of Bishop Alexander the Magnificent that he undertook the "*Historia Anglorum*," which he carried down to the year 1154.

The **North Aisle** has the double wall-arcade of St. Hugh on the one side, and the arcaded screens on the other. Three of the screens are of Grosseteste's time (1235-53); that in the easternmost bay is a slightly later work.

At the western end, an oak screen, carved with Gothic tracery and the linen pattern, separates the aisle from the chapel of St. James. The two westernmost piers on the south side shew the clumsy way in which they were restored after the fall of the central tower. On the side of the third pier is a carved head supporting a bracket in Purbeck marble.

The **Eastern Transept** is also the work of St. Hugh. There have been alterations made at a later period; these will be pointed out. The four semi-circular chapels on the east side were considered by Professor Willis to have been finished after the death of St. Hugh, though no doubt forming part of the original design. There hardly appears to be any necessity to assign them to a later date than the rest of the transept. The northern arm is in two bays, with the two semi-circular chapels on its eastern side, and a chamber, misnamed the "Dean's Chapel," to the west.

S. B. Bolas & Co., Photo.]

THE EAST TRANSEPT, LOOKING NORTH.

The end bay of the transept is cut off by an arch, carrying a wall above which reaches to the vault. The wall is pierced by openings similar to those of the triforium and clerestory, but they are unglazed, and through them we can see the windows of the outer wall. The compartment which this end bay thus forms has a stone vault at the height of the lower arch, leaving the part above open to the roof. Thus it happens that, looking [113] [114]

[115]from below through the upper openings, we are able to see right through to the massive wooden beams which support the outer roof. This is the only part of the interior from which the roof can be seen. It is interesting to notice the rows of windows in the north wall, culminating in the narrow lancets which fill the gable. The triforium is very similar to that of the choir. Each bay contains two arches, themselves divided into two sub-arches. The tympana are pierced, as before, with trefoils and quatrefoils, except in the case of the first bay on the eastern side, where they are plain. This is an interesting point, and is considered to mark the earliest existing part of St. Hugh's work. The clerestory is formed of narrow single lancets. The double arcading of St. Hugh is seen to the left of the doorway, in the north wall, which leads to the cloisters. Two columns of extraordinary design occur in this transept. One is at the south-east corner of the "Dean's Chapel," and the other is in a corresponding position on the other side of the church. Each consists of an octagonal pier in the centre, with crockets running up four of its sides; these are protected by four circular shafts of Purbeck marble, which stand before them and alternate with hexagonal fluted

shafts. The crockets form "a remarkable and uncommon feature, which seems to have been in use for a very few years; it occurs also in the west front of Wells Cathedral, the work of Bishop Joceline, a few years after this at Lincoln" (*Rickman*). The original purpose of the square chapel, constructed not long after the transept was built, is not known. Its name, the **Dean's Chapel**, appears to be given without reason. The oak door by which we enter from the transept has some fine hinges and bands of wrought ironwork, dating from the thirteenth century. The chamber was originally in two compartments, one above the other. The upper one was reached by a newel staircase to the north; this is now blocked up. The dividing floor has been removed, but the line may be traced on the walls, and the curious triangular-headed recesses above look like the cupboards of a dispensary. It has been suggested that the upper chamber served this purpose. There appears to be nothing which would give a clue as to the use to which the lower chamber was put. It is lit by two rough square-headed windows, cut in the double arcade of the western wall. The south window has still the original oak shutters, |116|with wrought-iron hinges and bands. The tie-beams of the east and south arches of the compartment still remain, and are now built up in the walls. The more northern of the semi-circular chapels is the one that was lengthened in the early part of the thirteenth century; the present eastern wall is entirely the work of James Essex, who, it will be remembered, reconstructed the chapel in 1772. It would be difficult to trace the history of this chapel. Whether it was dedicated to St. John the Baptist, and was consequently the original burial-place of St. Hugh, or whether it was (as Dugdale called it) the chapel of the Virgin Mary, is a question still undecided. 9 Like its neighbour, it is divided off from the transept by an oak screen carved with Gothic tracery (partly in openwork), and the linen pattern, constructed probably about the end of the fifteenth century. In the north wall there was originally a doorway, now walled up, leading into the Common Room. Fragments of the monument of Bishop Grosseteste, which stood in the south arm of the transept, are now stored away in this chapel. Each chapel has arcading round its walls, and is lit by two windows. On the wall which separates the "Dean's Chapel" from the transept are painted full-length figures of Robert Bloet and the three bishops who came after him— Alexander the Magnificent, Robert de Chesney, and Walter de Coutances. They are said to have been buried near here; if so, their tombs must have been removed from some other spot, as the transept was not built until a later period. They are marked in the plan of the year 1672 in Dugdale's "*Monasticon Anglicanum*." The bishops are represented beneath Gothic arches, and have their names inscribed above them. They were painted in the year 1728, by a Venetian artist named Vincenzo Damini, aided by his pupil, Giles Hussey (b. 1710: d. 1788). Two years later Hussey accompanied his master to Italy; Damini decamped at Bologna with all Hussey's property, and the latter was obliged to obtain relief from Signor Chislonzoni, a former Venetian ambassador in London. "Time," eighty years after, was "fast destroying the tints," and another eighty years has continued the work of destruction. From what still remains, it seems that it will be no great loss when the pictures are entirely effaced.

|117|

H. C. Oakden, Photo.]

TRIFORIUM ON THE WEST SIDE OF ST. HUGH'S TRANSEPT.

The southern arm of the transept has been considerably altered since it was first built. It is in two bays, with two apsidal chapels to the east, and the choristers' vestry and an ante-vestry to the west. At the south-west corner, the large square canons' vestry has been built out at a later period. There are indications which shew that the end bay was cut off by an arch, in the same way as the northern bay of the transept. These are noticeable in the column between the two apsidal chapels, and the lines of the original low vaulting of this end bay may still be traced on the south and west walls. When the arch and vault were removed, it would appear that the upper part of this end of the transept was rebuilt. The last bay of the triforium on the west has four narrow arches of equal height, whereas the adjoining bay does not differ from that in the northern arm. In the south wall there are two rows of three windows instead of two rows of two. The chief indications of a later date are, however, in the smaller details. Tooth ornament is used to a greater extent than in the |118|rest of the transept, and the wall spaces between the clerestory windows and the vault are covered with diaper work. This profusion of ornament would not be consistent with the time of St. Hugh. The alteration appears to have been made about the middle of the thirteenth century. Precentor Venables considered that its object was to throw a brighter light upon St. Peter's altar, which stood in the southern apsidal chapel, and was, next to the high altar, the chief altar in the church. The companion chapel has an oak screen with Gothic tracery, and a similar screen opposite divides the choristers' vestry from the transept. They both appear to date from about the end of the fifteenth century. The southern chapel has a low iron screen of modern workmanship. This chapel was the scene of the murder of Subdean William Bramfield or Bramford, by one of the vicars of the church, in 1205; the murderer was tied to the tail of a horse, dragged to Canwick Hill and there hanged. The recumbent effigy in marble of John Kaye, bishop of the diocese from 1827 to 1853, by Westmacott, is now placed in the chapel; it formerly stood in the transept, and was removed here for protection. At Cambridge, Kaye was Senior Wrangler, Senior Chancellor's Medallist, and Junior Smith's Prizeman. In 1814 he was appointed master of Christ's College; six years later he became Bishop of Bristol, whence he was transferred to Lincoln in 1827. The walls of both chapels are lined with arcading. The southern, unlike the other apsidal chapels, has three windows. The south wall of the transept has the double arcading, with figures of angels projecting from the small compartments formed by the intersecting arches.

The **Choristers' Vestry** occupies the corner nearest the south aisle of St. Hugh's choir, from which it is separated by a stone screen of the Decorated period, excellently carved on both sides with diaper designs. The screen reaches to the crocketed column before referred to. The long stone lavatory within the vestry appears to be of the same date as this screen, against which it is placed. Below the trough is a row of Gothic arcading. In the corner is an old fireplace, the stone flue of which can be seen outside. The double arcading along the west wall is less injured than elsewhere; the sculptured angels which fill the spaces formed by the intersecting arches are in fair preservation. Between this vestry |119| [120]

|121|and the canons' vestry are two narrow chambers, one of which is used as an ante-vestry. In the year 1805, between the 10th and the 15th January, the communion plate belonging to the cathedral was stolen out of one of the vestries. It consisted of one large dish, three plates, two large flagons, and two cups with covers, all of silver gilt. A reward was offered for their recovery, but without success.

S. B. Bolas & Co., Photo.]

NORTH SIDE OF THE ANGEL CHOIR.

A stone in the pavement in front of the chapel containing the effigy of Bishop Kaye, marks the position of the tomb of Grosseteste. Leland, in the time of Henry VIII., mentions that "Robert Grosted lyethe in the hygheste South Isle with a goodly Tumbe of Marble and an Image of Brasse over it." The monument was wrecked in the wars of the following century. Fragments of the stone canopy are still preserved; they are now deposited in the northernmost semi-circular chapel of this transept.

The general effect of the interior of the minster would undoubtedly have been better, had the original apse of St. Hugh still remained; the monotony of the continuous line of vaulting, carried to such a great length at an almost uniform height, would then have been avoided. But, taken by itself, there is no structure of modest dimensions in the whole range of Gothic architecture which is more beautiful in its details or more majestic in its effect than Lincoln's **Angel Choir**. Architecture and sculpture of the highest excellence are here united in a single work. Sir G. G. Scott in his Lectures on Mediæval Architecture, speaks of the angel choir in the following words:—"It is the most splendid work of that period which we possess, and, did it not lack internal height, I do not think it could be exceeded in beauty by any existing church." The period during which it was in great part erected (1256-1280) was favourable to such an undertaking. The primitive simplicity of the Early English Gothic was giving way to the more elaborate forms of the Decorated period. During this time, when tracery had not yet reached the flowing lines of the later phases of Decorated work, Gothic architecture, and in fact Gothic art generally, was at its best in our land. The angel choir was called by Fergusson "the most beautiful presbytery in England." It is in five bays, carried eastward at a uniform height and breadth with the choir of St. Hugh. Lincoln stone is used throughout; |122|relieved with shafts and capitals of Purbeck marble. A better idea of the piers can be gained from the accompanying illustration than from any description. The spandrels of the great arches, which are plain in other parts of the building, are here decorated with sunk geometrical forms. Each bay of the triforium is divided, as elsewhere, into two arches, both of which enclose two sub-arches; but the details are richer than in the earlier parts of the minster. The clerestory has one window of four lights in each bay, with an eight-foil and two trefoils in the head. The compartments of the vault were originally coated with plaster, which has been scraped away so as to shew the stone surface underneath. It is a question whether it does not now look better than with the old plaster, and the gaudy colouring which once, most probably, decorated it. The springers of the vaulting are supported by slender shafts, which rest on elaborately foliaged corbels in the spandrels of the great arches. The beautiful foliaged bosses along the ridge rib are best seen from the triforium or the clerestory.

The great east window is considered to be the finest example of its style in the kingdom. It is of eight lights, "formed by doubling the four-light," and has a great circle in the head, filled with a six-foil surrounded by half-a-dozen quatrefoils. "Bar-tracery being fully developed," we read in a note to Rickman's "Gothic Architecture," "the general appearance of the window is rather Decorated than Early English, but the mouldings still belong to the earlier style." "This window ... together with the whole of that part of the choir is singularly and beautifully accommodated to the style of the rest of the building."

The aisle windows are each of three lights, with three circles in the head, two filled with cinquefoils and one with a quatrefoil. The two east windows of the aisles are similar to the others. The wall below the windows is decorated all round with arcading of a richer design than that in the nave. Two trefoiled arches are included in a larger arch, with a quatrefoil within a circle filling the head. The spandrels have sunk trefoils. The bosses of the stone vaults to the aisles are carved with sacred subjects, foliage, and grotesque figures.

|123|

S. B. Bolas & Co., Photo.]

EAST END OF THE ANGEL CHOIR.

|124|

|125|

The sculptured angels, from which this part of the minster derives its name, fill the spandrels of the triforium, occupying a length of 118 feet on each side. It has been suggested that the idea may have been taken from the angels in St. Hugh's double wall-arcading, remains of which are still seen in different parts. The whole series has been fully illustrated, and exhaustively described and interpreted by Professor C. R. Cockerell, in the Lincoln volume (1848) of the Archæological Institute. Two hands of different merit are recognised by him in the work; he considers Nos. 4 to 18 (counting round from the south-east corner) to be amongst the best. The others are of inferior execution, though often of excellent design. They were carved before being placed in their present positions, as is evident from No. 11, the joints of which are not perfectly adjusted, and they are of the same stone as was employed in the architecture of the cathedral. Could it have been Richard of Stow or Gainsborough, the *cementarius*, who was employed to execute these sculptures?

THE LINCOLN IMP.
DRAWN BY H. P. CLIFFORD.

A description of Lincoln minster would not be complete without a reference to a small sculptured figure of vastly different character to the choir of angels—that delightfully grotesque little specimen of ugliness, known as the **Lincoln Imp**. He is to be seen on a spandrel on the north side, squatting under the corbel above the easternmost pier. The broad grin, the two short horns behind the ears, the hairy [126]body, and the cloven hoofs all combine to form a characteristic record of the exuberant fancy of our mediæval artists. The incised lines in the pavement of the south aisle, just where it joins the eastern transept, mark the position of the foundations of St. Hugh's apse. The first window in this aisle, just over Bishop Longland's chantry, is inscribed with the names and dates of the Chancellors of Lincoln. The series commences at the end of the eleventh century, and the last name recorded is "Edw. White Benson, S.T.P. 1872."

The east windows of the north and south aisles are filled with beautiful **stained glass** of the Early English period. The subjects are arranged within medallions, and, though somewhat difficult to decipher, appear to represent scenes in the lives of two saints whose story has many points of resemblance—St. Thomas of Canterbury and St. Hugh of Lincoln. The glass is said to have been moved about the end of the last century from the windows of the nave aisles. The date of the medallions may be placed towards the middle of the thirteenth century, about the time of the erection of the nave, and, of course, earlier than the windows which they now occupy. The *grisaille* into which they are now reglazed, is considered by Westlake to be the earliest in England.

The great east window is filled with modern glass. It is believed to have originally contained the arms of many of the English nobility. In the year 1762 it was reglazed by Peckitt of York; the design of that time seems to have been chiefly, if not entirely, of geometrical forms. Portions of Peckitt's glass now occupy a place in the north wall of the eastern transept. The arrangement of the subjects in the present window is due to the late Dean Ward. The compartments contain subjects illustrating the life of Christ, and various scenes from the Old Testament history. The window was executed by Ward and Hughes about the middle of the present century.

S. B. Bolas & Co., Photo.]

TRIFORIUM OF THE ANGEL CHOIR.

The three chantries in the Perpendicular style which have been added to the angel choir were constructed at different periods by bishops of the diocese. The earliest of these, the **Fleming Chantry**, is on the north side. Richard Fleming, the founder of Lincoln College, Oxford, was appointed Bishop of Lincoln in the year 1419, and occupied the see for twelve years. In earlier years he was known as a zealous supporter [127] [128]of many of the doctrines of Wyclif, but was afterwards called upon, as Bishop of Lincoln, to give effect to the council of Constance by exhuming the bones of the reformer from the churchyard at Lutterworth, burning them and casting them into the River Swift; "as the Swift bare them into the Severn, and the Severn into the narrow seas, and they again into the ocean, thus the ashes of Wycliffe is an emblem of his doctrine, which is now dispersed over all the world" (*Fuller*). The front of the chapel facing the choir is formed by a broad flat arch enclosing the founder's tomb, with a narrow entrance at the side. The door is of carved oak, with an ancient iron handle. On the tomb is the effigy of the bishop, restored not long since to this its original place. It presents a recumbent figure holding in the left hand a pastoral staff; the mitre is held by two angels, and at the bishop's feet is a dragon. Underneath is a horrible emaciated figure intended to represent the body of the bishop after death. Such figures are not uncommon; perhaps the best known example is in the choir of Canterbury Cathedral—the figure of Archbishop Chichele. Some authorities have considered that the figure at Lincoln does not represent Bishop Fleming, but that it formed part of an earlier monument. The chapel has been restored in memory of the late Sir Charles H. J. Anderson, Bart. (d. 1891), a native of Lincolnshire, and the author of an entertaining pocket guide to the county. The roof is of oak, carved with vine and oak foliage.

The **Russell chantry**, occupying a corresponding position on the opposite side of the choir, was built by Bishop John Russell, who held the see from 1480 to 1494. He is called by Sir Thomas More "a wise manne and a good ... and one of the best-learned men, undoubtedly, that England had in hys time." He was Chancellor of England under Richard III., and also held the post of Chancellor of Oxford University for some years. He died at

Nettleham in 1494. The chantry is similar in style to Bishop Fleming's; its roof is of oak. The incised brass of the tomb has gone the way of all the minster brasses. **Bishop Longland's chantry** is on the other side of the south door. The general design is an imitation of Bishop Russell's chantry, but the details are much more elaborate. Over the flat archway facing the choir is the punning inscription, "Longa Terra Mensura Eius Dominus Dedit," borrowed [129] from the Vulgate version of the book of Job (ch. xi., ver. 9). Round the inside walls of the chapel is an unfinished row of stone niches, with elaborately carved canopies; there is a panelled oak ceiling. This chapel was not erected until some time after the others; John Longland was Bishop of Lincoln from 1521 to 1547. He held, like Russell, the post of chancellor of the University of Oxford, but does not seem to have been very popular there, since on one occasion he was pelted with stones. When Henry VIII. visited Lincoln in 1541, he was received at the western end of the minster by this bishop, and stayed as his guest in the palace. Longland died in 1547, at Woburn, leaving instructions that his bowels were to be buried there; his heart at Lincoln; and his body in the chapel of Eton College. The building of the chapel at Lincoln seems to have been commenced soon after the bishop's accession to the see. Leland says "Byshope Russell, and Longland, now Byshop, Tumbes be in to Chapells cast out of the uppar Parte of the Southe Wall of the Churche." The chapel underwent a restoration in 1859.

The two chief **monuments** in the angel choir were the shrine of St. Hugh and the monument of Queen Eleanor. The former, of silver gilt, fell a victim to the royal greed of Henry VIII.; the latter, of more humble material, survived those perilous times, only to be destroyed by the rude soldiery of the Civil Wars in the seventeenth century. A description of the monument has, fortunately, been left to us by Bishop Sanderson, and the gilt brass effigy of the Queen in Westminster Abbey was the work of the same artist as that at Lincoln, and most probably a duplicate of it. Eleanor was the daughter of Ferdinand III. of Castile, and in 1254 was married to Henry III.'s eldest son, afterwards king as Edward I. Her attachment to her husband led her to accompany him on his adventurous expedition to the Holy Land with Louis IX. (St. Louis) of France in 1270. The king and queen seem to have travelled much together. They were both present at Lincoln at the translation of St. Hugh's relics in 1280, and ten years later, were again travelling northward, when Eleanor fell ill of a slow fever, and had to be lodged at Hardeby (Harby), just within the borders of Nottinghamshire. Lincoln was five miles off, and medicines were procured in the city from Henry de Montepessulano, to whom the sum of 13s. 4d. was paid. [130] These remedies, however, proved of no effect, and on the 28th November 1290 the queen died, in the presence of her husband. Her body was embalmed and carried to Lincoln, where the viscera were buried in the minster, and a noble monument was raised. On the 4th December, the funeral procession left Lincoln, and journeyed to London. The heart, at the queen's own desire, was deposited in the church of the Friars Predicants in London, and the body was buried in Westminster Abbey on the 17th December, the Bishop of Lincoln officiating. There the monument was raised which still exists. The famous crosses, twelve in number, were erected at the different places on the route where the body rested for a night, doubtless in imitation of those in memory of the king's old crusader friend. St. Louis had died at Tunis, and the body was taken back to Paris, whence it was borne on the shoulders of men to the venerable resting-place of the French kings at St. Denis. Crosses were erected where the bearers rested in the journey from Paris to St Denis.

The first of the Eleanor crosses was at Lincoln, and there are records of payments to the "cementarius" Richard de Stow for the work. The last was at Charing. With reference to the monument in Lincoln minster, we learn from Bishop Sanderson's description that it was an altar monument of marble, "whereon was a Queen's effigies in gilded brass," and had the following inscription in "Saxon" characters:—*Hic sunt Sepulta viscera Alienorae quondam Reginae Angliae uxoris Regis Edwardi filii Regis Henrici, cujus animae propicietur Deus.—Amen.* The marble tomb was executed by Dymenge de Legeri and Alexander de Abyngton, who received £25 for the work; Roger de Crundale had £1, 16s. 8d. for marble; William de Suffolk was paid 8 marks for three little images of the queen, cast in metal, to be placed near the tomb. William de Suffolk also produced some small images for the church of the Friars Predicants in London. The effigies of the queen both at Westminster and Lincoln, were cast by Master

William Torel, goldsmith and citizen of London. For the gilding, Flemish coin were procured from the merchants of Lucca.

A modern stone monument, with a bronze effigy of Queen Eleanor on the top, has recently (in 1891) been placed under the great east window, near the Cantelupe monument. It is [131]due to the munificence of Mr. Joseph Ruston, and is a copy, as near as one can now tell, of the original monument. In the north-east corner of the choir is a group of monuments to a family which derived its name from Burghersh or Burwash in Sussex. Here was the chantry of St. Catherine, founded by Bartholomew, Lord Burghersh, for the soul of his brother Henry and their father, Robert Burghersh. The chaplains lived in the Burghersh chantry house in James Street. Leland, in referring to the "Burwasche" family, says that "they foundyd 5. Prists, and 5. pore Scollars at Gramar Schole in Lyncolne." Henry Burghersh was Bishop of Lincoln from 1320 to 1340. He was the third or fourth son of Sir Robert Burghersh, Lord Burghersh. Like many of our mediæval bishops, he appears to have been much more of a statesman than an ecclesiastic. For some time he was Chancellor of England under Edward III., whose son, the Black Prince, he baptised. He was a principal adviser of the king in foreign affairs, and died at Ghent in the year 1340, while there engaged in business of State. The monument is of stone, with a fine recumbent effigy of the bishop on the top, now much defaced. His mitre is supported by two angels. Along the north side of the monument runs an arcade of five arches, within each of which are two seated figures, whose armorial shields appear in the spandrels above. First (at the head) is Edward III.; then follow his four sons: Edward, the Black Prince, Lionel, Duke of Clarence, John of Gaunt, and Edmund, Duke of York; next is Henry, Duke of Lancaster, whose daughter, Blanche, married John of Gaunt. The other effigies are those of persons allied with the Burghersh family. On the other side of the monument are four panels of Gothic tracery with shields of arms. The legend runs that at Tinghurst, in Buckinghamshire, Bishop Henry Burghersh, "by mere might against all right and reason," enclosed the land of many poor people, without recompense, in order to complete his park. The ghost of the bishop could not rest after his death, but appeared to the canons of Lincoln in hunting dress, telling them he was appointed keeper of the park, and beseeching them to throw it open. The canons, thus warned, restored the land to its rightful possessors.

Next to this is another Burghersh monument, which authorities do not seem to be quite agreed about. Leland, after speaking [132]of the bishop's tomb, says: "there is also buried at his Fete, Robart,*his Brothar*, a Knighte of great Fame in the Warrs." But the general opinion seems to be that Robert was not the brother, but the father, of Henry and Bartholomew. This tomb is of similar style to the former, having figures beneath arches on one side, and shields of arms on the other. The effigy is gone from the top. The elaborate Gothic canopies which originally surmounted both tombs were much injured by boys clambering upon them, and, becoming unsafe at last, were removed in the early part of the present century. Against the opposite wall, within a recessed arch under the easternmost window, is the monument of Henry's elder brother, Bartholomew, Lord Burghersh (d. 1355)—a soldier of much renown, who had a share in the victory of Creçy. He held the important office of constable of Dover Castle and warden of the Cinque Ports. In the year 1329, he was sent on a mission to the Pope to plead for pecuniary aid from the revenues of the English church; a tenth of them was granted to the king for four years. The base of the monument has an arcade of six arches, each having two small pedestals, for figures which are now gone. The armorial shields of the persons originally represented beneath the arches still remain in the spandrels. The effigy shows him clad in plate armour, and reclining on his helmet; two angels at the head uphold the shield of his family, and two others at the foot bear away in a cloth the deceased warrior's soul. The canopy over the tomb bears the arms of Edward III. and his four sons (the same as on the tomb of his brother the bishop), together with the shield of Thomas, Earl of Lancaster and Lincoln. A detailed account of the shields of arms on the Burghersh tombs may be found in the Lincoln volume (1848) of the Archæological Institute.

H. C. Oakden, Photo.]

TOMB OF SIR BARTHOLOMEW BURGERSH.

Joined on to the end of Bishop Burghersh's tomb is the lofty base of a portable shrine. It has three niches, two on the north side and one in the front, for worshippers to kneel in. Over the arches are shields bearing the Instruments of the Passion. It is apparently of the same date as the bishop's monument. The old pavement slab, worn away by the feet of those who visited the shrine, has been left in front. Opposite to the Burghersh monuments, just to the south of the great east window, is the monument of Nicholas de Cantelupe, third Baron Cantelupe, who died in 1355. This warrior was much [133] [134]

[135]occupied in the wars of Edward II. and his successor, Edward III. He founded Cantelupe College, a college of priests to celebrate at the altar of St. Nicholas, 10 which stood near the tomb, at the eastern end of the south aisle. Baron Cantelupe's widow, Joan, enlarged the foundation, and probably built the Cantelupe chantry house in the minster yard. The effigy, in armour, is now headless and legless. Round the base, on the south and west sides, are shields of arms in panels, which shew traces of colouring. The monument has a lofty Gothic canopy. Just westward is buried Prior Wimbische (or Wymbysh, d. 1478) "in a fayre Highe Tombe." This monument, like the adjoining one, has shields of arms on the base, and a rich canopy above; the effigy is headless.

Near these tombs, at the south-east corner of the choir, is the monument to William Hilton, R.A. (b. 1786: d. 1839), and his brother-in-law, the famous water-colour painter, Peter De Wint (b. 1784: d. 1849). Hilton lived in a house, still standing, not far from the minster. His friend De Wint greatly loved the level plains of Lincolnshire and the surrounding country, and no artist was better able to depict its peculiar charms. The minster was one of his favourite subjects, and he painted it from several different points. The principal of these is a large water-colour in the South Kensington Museum, taken from near the castle gateway (see illustration, p. 33). The ancient houses seen near the Exchequer Gate are an interesting record of old Lincoln. The marble relief on the west side of the monument is copied from this picture. On the front are three marble reliefs from pictures by Hilton— the Woman with the alabaster box of ointment, the Crucifixion and the Raising of Lazarus. They are signed "I. Forsyth sculp." The monument is of stone, with Gothic tracery, and has four kneeling angels at the corners. It was erected in the year 1864 by the bereaved sister and widow, Harriet De Wint.

Across the middle of the choir, just behind the reredos, is a row of four table-tombs. The first of these, to the north, was erected by Bishop Fuller soon after the Restoration, to mark the supposed burial-place of Bishop St. Hugh. The [136]saint's shrine was in the centre of the choir, but it is supposed that when the shrine was melted down the body was removed and placed somewhere else, perhaps in this spot marked by Bishop Fuller. The tomb was opened in the year 1886, when the stone coffin was found to contain nothing but decaying vestments. In Leland's time, St. Hugh lay "in the Body of the Est Parte of the Chirche above the Highe Altare." The next monument is that of Bishop Fuller himself, who was summoned *ex ultimâ Hiberniâ*, as the epitaph records, to preside over the See of Lincoln. William Fuller was a chaplain of Christ Church Catedral, Oxford, but, as a steady Royalist, lost his post during the war. At the Restoration he was rewarded with the deanery of St. Patrick's, Dublin, and became soon after Bishop of Limerick. In the year 1667 the bishopric of Lincoln was vacant. There were two candidates for the appointment, Dr. Glenham, Dean of Bristol, and Dr. Rainbow, Bishop of Carlisle. Fuller, hearing of this, suggested that the difficulty should be solved by his own transference from Limerick to Lincoln, and his suggestion was carried out. Pepys, a friend of Fuller's, mentions the fact with delight. The new bishop did his utmost to repair the injuries perpetrated during the Civil War. He restored many monuments, and was meditating other works in the same direction, when he died at Kensington, 23rd April 1675. The third monument is that of Bishop Gardiner, who presided over the see for ten years, dying in March 1704-5. This bishop, in a visitation of the diocese, found a bad state of affairs in several churches where the chancels were disused and left "in a more nasty condition than the meanest cottage," while the holy table was brought down into the mid-aisle. The Latin inscriptions on the monuments of Bishops Fuller and Gardiner are somewhat quaint. The last of the four monuments is that of Subdean Gardiner (d. 1731-2), and his only daughter Susanna, who died a year later. Near the monument of Bishop Gardiner is a slab in the pavement, marking the tomb of "Michael Honywood, D.D., who was grandchild and one of the 367 persons that Mary, the wife of Robert Honywood Esq., did see before she dyed lawfully descended from her." The elaborate stone monument in the third bay on the north side is in memory of Bishop Wordsworth (b. 1807: d. 1885), a nephew of the poet. The base is decorated with Gothic [137]arcading, and has figures of the twelve apostles. On it rests the recumbent effigy of the bishop, clad in a cope and mitre. At his head are two angels, and a dragon lies beneath his feet. Above is a lofty and intricate Gothic canopy, with a figure of Christ in the centre.

A monument to Dean Butler (d. 1894) has recently been placed near the tomb of Subdean Gardiner. It is of alabaster and red marble, with a recumbent effigy of the dean, who is buried in the cloister garth.

In the next bay eastward is a slab which marks the burial-place of Oliver Sutton (bishop of the diocese from 1280 to 1299), by whom the cloisters were built. The slab, of Purbeck marble, was raised in the year 1889 by workmen engaged in repairing the pavement. Beneath was an oblong stone chest, lined with sheets of lead, enclosing the skeleton of the bishop, which lay in a mass of decaying vestments. On the right side of the skeleton a silver-gilt chalice was found, with a paten laid upon it, covered with a piece of fine linen. The chalice stands 4-½ in. high, with a broad shallow bowl, 4 in. in diameter. The foot is circular, of the same diameter as the bowl, and the knop projects ½ in. from the stem. It is entirely destitute of ornament. The paten is 4-¾ in. in diameter, with the *Manus Dei* in the act of benediction, issuing from conventional clouds. The large finger-ring of the bishop was also discovered. It is of pure gold, with a massive hoop; a large piece of rock-crystal is set in the oval bezel. These extremely interesting relics are preserved in the Cathedral Library, where are also the rings of Bishops Gravesend and Grosseteste. On the left side of the skeleton lay the mouldering remains of a wooden crozier, carved with leaf ornament. In the north aisle is buried Robert Dymoke (d. 1735), a member of the ancient family who held for nearly five centuries the office of King's Champion. It was the champion's duty to ride on his horse into Westminster Hall at the coronation banquet, and three times to challenge to combat any person who disputed the sovereign's title. A member of this family, Henry Dymoke, acted as champion at the coronation of George IV. (19th July 1821), the last occasion on which this custom was observed.

The **Cloisters** are reached by a doorway in the north [138]wall of the eastern transept. The door is of oak, with some ancient wrought ironwork scrolls on the outer side. A narrow barred window over the door lights a small room anciently used as a watching-chamber. A long, narrow vestibule leads to the cloisters; it has a stone vault, rendered conspicuous by modern colouring; the bosses are carved with foliage and figures. The windows are filled with tracery similar to that in the cloisters, but they are glazed, as the cloister windows probably were originally.

H. C. Oakden, Photo.]

BISHOP WORDSWORTH'S TOMB.

S. B. Bolas & Co., Photo.]

THE CLOISTERS, FROM THE NORTH-EAST CORNER.

The cloisters are in an unusual position; they were generally built on the south side of the church, against the wall of the nave, where they would be protected from the cold north and east winds. At Lincoln they are on the north side, opposite the choir, and stand away from [139]
[140]

[141]the walls of the church. Lincoln had no need of cloisters, any more than York or

Lichfield, all three being secular churches. There seems to have been no idea of their erection before the end of the thirteenth century. The colonnade which has taken the place of the north walk, together with the Library above it, was erected from the designs of Sir Christopher Wren in 1674. The cost was paid by Dean Honywood, who also gave to the chapter his collection of books.

ARCADE IN THE CHAPTER-HOUSE.

An account of the contents the **Library** is given by Beriah Botfield in his "Notes on the Cathedral Libraries of England" (1849). The MS. library includes several Latin Bibles and Psalters, as well as a most valuable MS. of Old English Romances, c. 1430-40, collected by Robert de Thornton, who was Archdeacon of Bedford in 1450, and lies buried in Lincoln Cathedral. Some time between the years 1816 and 1828, all the Caxtons and many early volumes were sold, the proceeds being devoted to the purchase of more modern works of which the Library stood in need. A number of useful books were thus added to the collection, but only by the sacrifice of works which it would be quite impossible to replace. At the time of Botfield's visit, the library contained 4451 volumes, relating to theological, classical and historical subjects. Among the English versions of the Bible were found Tyndale's, Coverdale's, Cranmer's, Matthew's, the Bishops' Bible and the Genevan Bible. The library contains a portrait, said to be by Cornelis Janssens, of its great benefactor. The authorship of this painting is very doubtful, since Janssens left England in 1648, and Honywood was dean from 1660 to 1681.

[142]

CAPITAL IN THE CHAPTER-HOUSE.

The inside measurement of the cloisters is 120 feet from east to west, and 90 feet from north to south. In the middle of the south walk there is a doorway in the wall. A good view of the north side of St. Hugh's choir, the side walls of the transepts, and the central tower, can be had from the doorway. An old cast lead cistern in the corner is worth noticing. It is cylindrical, with bands of vine-stems in relief. In the wall to the left of the door are the fragments of the monumental slab of Richard of Gainsborough (d. 1300). He is probably the same man as Richard of Stow (a village not far from Gainsborough), who was engaged on the carved work of the angel choir, and was also employed on the crosses in memory of Queen Eleanor. On the other side of the door is a restoration of the slab in plaster, and another restoration is in the pavement. The mason, with a carpenter's square by his side, is represented beneath a Gothic canopy; around is the inscription "Hic jacet Ricardus de Gaynisburgh olym cementarius istius ecclesie qui obiit duodecim kalendarum junii Anno domini MCCC."

In the north walk beneath the library is the original Swineherd of Stow, which for many centuries crowned the northern turret of the west front. A modern copy has now taken its place. At the east end of the walk, near the library staircase, are several fragments of ancient carving, chiefly of the Norman period. A stone coffin, carved with interlacing circles, probably goes back to Saxon times. From this point may be had the best view of the north end of the great transept, with its fine round window. Some interesting relics of Roman Lincoln are placed on the floor at the foot of the library staircase; they have been described by Precentor Venables.

Along the east walk of the cloisters is a row of wall-arcading, with Purbeck shafts and tooth ornament.

[143]

Photochrom Co. Ltd., Photo.]

THE CHAPTER-HOUSE.

The vault of the three ancient walks is of oak, with stone springers. There is a fine series of oak bosses, carved with figures, grotesque heads, animals and foliage. An interesting set of photographs was taken from these bosses when the cloister was in process of reconstruction a few years ago; they are reproduced in the *Builder* of July 19th, 1890. In the cloister garth are the tombs of Dean Butler (to whose memory a monument has recently been placed in the angel [144]choir) and his wife, and Precentor Venables (d. 1895) and his daughter. The late precentor will be long remembered by those who are interested in the history of the minster; the results of his patient investigations, published chiefly in the *Archæological Journal*, cannot fail to be of great service to any who are desirous of information with respect to the architecture of the minster, or the antiquities of the city. The cloisters still bear marks of the rough usage they received in the last century, when they served the purpose of sheds for scaffolding and building materials. The doorway opening into the vestibule of the chapter-house is in the east walk. The oak door is a gift of the present bishop (Dr. King). Over the door inside is an arcade of slender arches with a large round window above, which would look better filled with coloured glass.

The **Chapter-house** is one of the earliest of the series of polygonal chapter-houses in England, dating from the early part of the thirteenth century. It is a decagon with two windows in each bay; nearly all of these have now been filled with stained glass, in memory of different dignitaries connected with the minster. The glass is by Clayton and Bell, and deals with the history of the minster from its foundation. Below the windows an arcade runs right round the walls, with Purbeck shafts, foliaged capitals (see page 142), and a profusion of tooth ornament. Below the arcading is a projecting stone seat. The stone vault is a little later than the rest of the chapter-house. It is supported by a cluster of shafts, against the wall, in each angle, resting on corbels carved with foliage. Besides these, there is a massive central column, surrounded by ten hexagonally-fluted Purbeck shafts, banded in the middle. Greater experience was necessary before the Gothic architects were able, as at York, to dispense with this central pillar, and to produce a perfect Gothic dome of such large dimensions. A corbel, carved with oak foliage, formerly supporting a figure of the Virgin Mary, is attached to the eastern side of this central column. In front of this is a socket in the pavement for holding a processional cross. The dean's chair, at one time in the library, is a fine piece of early fourteenth-century carved woodwork. On the arms are crouching lions; the front panel below the seat is carved with rows of quatrefoils. The canopy over the chair is modern. The chapter-house was restored under the directions of the late consulting architect to the chapter, J. L. Pearson, R.A.

[145]

CHAPTER IV
LIST OF THE BISHOPS OF LINCOLN

Remigius—Rémi—(1067-1092), Almoner of Fécamp, in Normandy; made Bishop of Dorchester by William the Conqueror, and soon after transferred the see to Lincoln.

Robert Bloet (1094-1123), brother of Hugh, Bishop of Bayeux; Chancellor of England under William the Conqueror and William Rufus; Justiciary under Henry I.

Alexander—"the Magnificent"—(1123-1148), nephew of Roger, Bishop of Salisbury; Archdeacon of Sarum, 1121; rebuilt chancel of St. Mary's at Stow; bequeathed certain books of the Bible to the Dean and Chapter; gatehouse of Eastgate in Lincoln granted to him as an episcopal residence by Henry I.

Robert de Chesney (1148-1166), Archdeacon of Leicester; founded Gilbertine priory of St. Catherine outside south Bar-gate; bought site for episcopal residence at Lincoln in 1155, and commenced building palace; purchased previous to 1162 "The Old Temple" in parish of St. Andrew's, Holborn, as London residence of bishops.

The see was vacant until 1173, when Geoffrey Plantagenet, natural son of Henry II., was appointed. He was never consecrated, although he retained the temporalities for nine years.

Walter de Coutances—de Constantiis—(1183-1184), Vice-Chancellor of England, Canon and Treasurer of Rouen Cathedral, 1173; Archdeacon of Oxford, 1175; translated to Rouen, 1184; d. 1207.

See vacant, 1184-1186.

Hugh of Avalon—St. Hugh of Lincoln—(1186-1200), Procurator of monastery of the Grande Chartreuse, 1170; Prior of Carthusian monastery at Witham, in Somerset, 1175-6 to 1186; commenced the great hall in the bishop's palace at Lincoln.

[146]

William de Blois (1203-1206).

See vacant, 1206-1209.

Hugh de Wells (1209-1235), Prebendary of Louth in the Cathedral, 1203; Archdeacon of Wells, 1204; built kitchen and completed hall in bishop's palace at Lincoln; also built manor-house at Buckden.

Robert Grosseteste (1235-1253), Archdeacon of Wilts, 1214 and 1220; of Northampton, 1221; first Rector of Franciscans at Oxford, 1224; Prebendary of Empingham in the Cathedral, afterwards exchanged for Archdeaconry of Leicester.

Henry de Lexinton (1253-1258), Treasurer of Salisbury, 1241; Prebendary of North Muskham at Southwell previous to 1242; Dean of Lincoln, 1245.

Richard de Gravesend (1258-1279), Dean of Lincoln, 1254; Treasurer of Hereford previous to 1258; absent from diocese about 1267-1269, when John de Maidenstone was in charge.

Oliver Sutton (1280-1299), Dean of Lincoln; built the cloisters.

John de Dalderby (1300-1320), Canon of St. David's; Archdeacon of Carmarthen, 1283; Chancellor of Lincoln, 1293; one of the Commissioners in 1309 in proceedings against the Knights Templars. (Dalderby is a village in Lincolnshire.)

Henry Burghersh (1320-1340), Prebendary of Riccall, in York Minster, 1316; Treasurer and Chancellor of England, 1328; deprived of chancellorship, 1330; re-elected Treasurer, 1334; dismissed, 1337; obtained right of sanctuary for bishop's palace and canons' houses at Lincoln.

Thomas Bek (1341—Feb. 1346-7), Doctor of Canon Law; Prebendary of Clifton in the Cathedral, 1335.

John Gynwell (1347-1362), Archdeacon of Northampton.

John Buckingham—Bokyngham—(1363-1397), Prebendary of Lichfield and Dean, 1349; Archdeacon of Northampton, 1351; Prebendary of Gretton in the Cathedral, 1352; Keeper of Privy Seal to Edward III.; translated to Lichfield, 1397; retired to monastery of Christ Church at Canterbury; d. 1398.

Henry Beaufort (1398-1404), Prebendary of Thame, 1389; of Sutton in the Cathedral, 1391; Dean of Wells, 1397; translated to Winchester, 1404; d. 1447.

[147]

Philip Repyngdon—Repington—(1405-1419), Augustinian Canon of St. Mary de Pré, Leicester, previous to 1382; excommunicated for Wiclifite heresy, July 1382; abjured, Nov. 1382; Abbot of St. Mary de Pré, 1391; Chancellor of Oxford University, 1397, 1400-1402; Chaplain and Confessor to Henry IV.; Cardinal, 1408; resigned, 1419; d. 1424.

Richard Fleming (1419—Jan. 1430-1), Prebendary of Langtoft, in York Minster, 1415; Rector of Boston; founder of Lincoln College, Oxford.

William Gray (1431-1436), Bishop of London, 1426-1431.

William of Alnwick (1436-1449), Keeper of the Privy Seal; Archdeacon of Salisbury; Bishop of Norwich, 1426-1436; built east wing of bishop's palace at Lincoln, with chapel and dining-parlour and a gateway tower.

Marmaduke Lumley (Jan. 1449-50—Dec. 1450), Treasurer of England; Chancellor of Cambridge University; Precentor of Lincoln, 1425; exchanged for rectory of Stepney, 1427; Bishop of Carlisle, 1430—Jan. 1449-50.

John Chadworth (1452-1471).

Thomas Rotherham—Scot—(1472-1480), Archdeacon of Canterbury, 1467; Bishop of Rochester, 1468-1472; translated to York, 1480; d. 1500; second founder of Lincoln College, Oxford.

John Russell (1480-1494), Archdeacon of Berkshire, 1466; Bishop of Rochester, 1476-1480; first of "perpetual Chancellors" of Oxford.

William Smyth (1496-1514), Bishop of Coventry and Lichfield, 1493-1496; co-founder of Brasenose College, Oxford, with Richard Button.

Thomas Wolsey (1514), Dean of Lincoln, 1508; Canon of Windsor; Dean of York; translated to Winchester and York, 1514; Cardinal, 1515; Papal Legate and Lord Chancellor, 1516; d. 1530.

William Atwater (1514—Feb. 1520-1), Chancellor of Lincoln, 1506-1512; Prebendary, Oct. 1512.

John Longland (1521-1547), Confessor to King Henry VIII.; Prebendary of Lincoln; built chantry chapel in Cathedral,

Henry Holbeach—Rands—(1547-1551), Prior of Worcester, 1536; Suffragan Bishop of Bristol to see of Worcester, 1538-1540; Dean of Worcester, 1540; Bishop of Rochester, 1544-1547.

[148]

John Taylor (1552-1554), deprived by Queen Mary.

John White (1554-1556), Prebendary of Winchester; translated to Winchester, 1556; deprived by Queen Elizabeth, 1559.

Thomas Watson (1557-1559), Dean of Durham; deprived by Queen Elizabeth.

Nicholas Bullingham (Jan. 1559-60—Jan. 1570-1), translated to Worcester, Jan. 1570-1; d. 1576.

Thomas Cooper—Couper—(1570-1—1584), Dean of Christ Church, Oxford, 1566; Vice-Chancellor of the University; Dean of Gloucester, 1569; translated to Winchester, 1584; d. 1594.

William Wickham (1584-1594), Dean of Lincoln; translated to Winchester, 1594; d. 1595.

William Chaderton—Chatterton—(1595-1608), President of Queen's College, Cambridge, 1568; Archdeacon of York; Prebendary of Westminster, 1576; Bishop of Chester, 1579-1595; resided at Southoe.

William Barlow (1608-1613), Bishop of Rochester, 1605-1608.

Richard Neile (1614-1617), Bishop of Rochester, 1608-1610; of Lichfield and Coventry, 1610-1614; of Durham, 1617-1627; of Winchester, 1627-1631; Archbishop of York, 1631-1640; d. 1640.

George Montaigne—Mountain—(1617-1621), Dean of Westminster, 1610; translated to London, 1621; to Durham, Feb. 1627-8; to York, July 1628; d. Oct. 1628.

John Williams (1621-1641), Dean of Westminster and Salisbury; Precentor of Lincoln; Lord Keeper under James I.; translated to York, 1641; d. 1650.

Thomas Winniffe (1642-1654). Bishop's palace at Lincoln demolished during this episcopacy.

Robert Sanderson (1660-1663), Regius Professor at Oxford, 1642 and 1660; restored episcopal residence of Buckden at his own cost; transcribed monumental inscriptions in the Cathedral.

Benjamin Laney (1663-1667), Vice-Chancellor of Cambridge University, 1632-1633; Dean of Rochester, July 1660; Bishop of Peterborough, Dec. 1660-1663; translated to Ely, 1667; d. Jan. 1674-5.

William Fuller (1667-1675), Dean of St. Patrick's, Dublin, July 1660; [149]Bishop of Limerick, Mar. 1663-4—1667; repaired damage done to the Cathedral, and restored monuments of Remigius and St. Hugh, supplying epitaphs; bequeathed books to Cathedral library.

Thomas Barlow (1675-1691), buried at Buckden.

Thomas Tenison (1691-1694), Archdeacon of London; translated to Canterbury, 1694; d. 1715.

James Gardiner (Mar. 1694-5—Mar. 1704-5), Sub-Dean of Lincoln, 1671; rebuilt episcopal residence, ruined by storming of Castle and Close in 1644.

William Wake (1705-1715), Dean of Exeter; translated to Canterbury, 1715; d. 1737.

Edmund Gibson (1716-1723), Archdeacon of Surrey, 1710; translated to London, 1723; d. 1748.

Richard Reynolds (1723—Jan. 1743-4), Dean of Peterborough, 1718; Bishop of Bangor, Dec. 1721-1723.

John Thomas (1744-1761), translated to Salisbury, 1761; d. 1766.

John Green (1761-1779), Dean of Lincoln and Vice-Chancellor of Cambridge, 1756; Resident Canon of St. Paul's Cathedral, 1771.

Thomas Thurlow (1779-1787).

George Pretyman Tomline, baronet (1787-1820), translated to Winchester, 1820; d. 1827.

George Pelham (1820-1827), Resident Canon of Chi-chester Cathedral, 1790; Prebendary of Winchester, 1797-1803; Bishop of Bristol, 1803-1807; of Exeter, 1807-1820.

John Kaye (1827-1853), Vice-Chancellor of Cambridge University, 1815; Bishop of Bristol, 1820-1827; resided at old palace of Buckden until 1837, when he removed to the newly-erected palace at Riseholme.

John Jackson (1853-1868), Canon of Bristol, 1853; translated to London, 1868; d. 1885.

Christopher Wordsworth (1868-1885), Headmaster of Harrow School, 1836-1844; Archdeacon of Westminster, 1865; resided at Riseholme.

Edward King (1885), Bishop's palace at Lincoln restored to its ancient use.

DIMENSIONS.

Total Interior Length—482 feet.

Nave—Length to Screen, 252 feet. Width, including Aisles, 80 feet. Height of Vault, 82 feet.

Choir—Length, 158 feet. Height of Vault, 74 feet.

Presbytery—Length, 72 feet. Height of Vault, 74 feet.

West Transept—Length, 222 feet. Width, 61 feet.

East Transept—Length, 170 feet. Width, 36 feet.

Central Tower—Height, 271 feet. Height of Vault, 125 feet.

West Towers—Height about 200 feet.

Chapter-house—Diameter, 60 feet.

AREA—44,400 square feet.